Advanced Stories for Reproduction

AMERICAN SERIES

L. A. HILL

Oxford University Press
外 國 語 研 修 社

Oxford University Press

OXFORD LONDON GLASGOW NEW YORK
TORONTO MELBOURNE WELLINGTON CAPE TOWN
IBADAN NAIROBI DAR ES SALAAM LUSAKA ADDIS ABABA
KUALA LUMPUR SINGAPORE JAKARTA HONG KONG
TOKYO DELHI BOMBAY CALCUTTA MADRAS KARACHI

First Korean impression 1985

Illustrations by Anna Veltfort

This book is available in the United States
in an alternate edition entitled
Advanced Anecdotes in American English.

ISBN 0-19-502770-1 (East Asia Edition)
ISBN 0-19-502603-9 (U.S. Edition)

Printed in Korea

영어의 표현력 및 이해력 양성에 역점을 둔 L. A. HILL 박사의
명저 Stories for Reproduction 총서 한국판을 내놓으면서

우리의 국력이 크게 신장되어 국제 교류의 폭이 확대되어 감에 따라 각계 각층에서 영어에 능통한 인재의 요구가 날로 늘어가고 있읍니다. 그러나 이러한 실력을 갖춘 인재는 구하기가 쉽지 않을 뿐 아니라, 최고 학부를 나온 분들 마저 영어를 필요로 하는 업무에 부닥치면 표현력(말과 글로 표현하기)이나 이해력(읽거나 듣고 이해하기) 부족 때문에 많은 곤란을 겪고 있읍니다.

따지고 보면 이러한 현상이 생기게 된 것은 당연한 결과라고 할 수 있겠읍니다. 왜냐하면 지금까지의 영어 교육이 난해한 영문의 국역이나 까다로운 문법체계의 학습에 치중한 나머지 작문력, 회화력, 독해력 특히 속독력 및 청해력 등을 양성하는 학습을 소홀히 해 왔기 때문입니다.

그렇다면 영어의 표현력과 이해력을 기르기 위해서는 무엇부터 시작하여 어떻게 해야 하는지 그 구체적인 방법을 살펴 보기로 합시다.

1. 상용 2000 단어의 철저한 학습과 활용

영어로 일상적인 의사표시를 하는 데 있어서는 빈도수가 높은 것만을 뽑아 만든 2,000 상용 단어만의 사용으로 부족함이 없읍니다. 예를 들면 6만의 표제어와 6만 9천의 예문을 싣고 있는 Longman Dictionary of Contemporary English는 표제어의 정의와 그 예문을 제시하는 데 2,000의 「정의 어휘(Defining Vocabulary)」와 단순한 문법구조만을 쓰고 있으며, Longman Dictionary of Business English도 Michael West의 상용 영어 단어 일람표(A General Service List of English Words)를 토대로 한 2,000여 단어와 단순한 문법구조만으로 Business 각 분야의 전문용어를 완벽하게 해설하고 있읍니다.

이런 사실만을 보아도 영어 실력 양성에 있어서 2,000 상용 단어의 철저한 학습과 그 활용연습이 얼마나 중요한 것이라는 것을 쉽게 이해할 수 있을 것입니다.

그럼에도 불구하고 이 2,000 상용 단어의 철저한 기초학습이 채 끝나기도 전에, 일상적 의사표시에는 별로 쓰이지 않아 기억하기도 힘든 많은 어려운 영어 단어들(고교 수준에서는 약 5,000, 대학과 대학원 수준에서는 10,000~30,000 단어)을 단편적, 기계적으로 암기하거나 난해한 영문의 국역이나 까다로운 문법체계의 학습에만 매달린다면 아무리 노력을 해 봤자 모래 위에 성을 쌓는 격이어서, 영어로 자신의 생각을 자유롭게 표현할 수 있는 정도까지 그 실력이 향상되기를 기대할 수 없는 것입니다.

2. 문맥적 접근법(Contextualized Approach)

어학의 습득은 「의미내용」의 「기억, 재현」과정을 통해 이루어지는 것이며, 이「의미내용」을 전달하는 효율은 1. 숫자(Figure) 2. 문자(Letter) 3. 단어(Word) 4. 문(Sentence) 5. 문장의 절(Paragraph)순으로, 그것이 함축하는 「의미내용」의 차원이 높은 것일수록 그 전달량이 커지고 전달 효율이 높아집니다. 따라서 영어 학습에 있어서도 단어나 문법을 따로 학습하는 것보다는 문장내에서 문맥(Context)에 따라 이를 학습하는 것이 그 기억과 재현의 효율을 높일 수 있는 것입니다.

3. 표현력 향상을 위한 재현(Reproduction)연습

영어의 표현력을 기르는 데는 모범적인 영어 문장을 되풀이해서 읽고 이것을 재현(Reproduction)하는 연습을 해 보는 것이 가장 효과적이라는 것은 이미 널리 알려진 사실입니다. 그래서 중·고교의 교과서를 한 권이라도 암기해 보라고 권유하는 분들이 많으나, 이 교과서 자체가 암기와 재현 연습용으로 쓰기에는, 본문의 길이가 너무 길거나 난해할 뿐 아니라 재현 연습을 유도하는 적절한 Questions, Exercises 및 Answer Key 등의 뒷받침이 되어 있지 않기 때문에 표현력 향상을 위한 교재로는 적합하지 못합니다.

영어 교육계의 오랜 경험에서 밝혀진 바에 의하면 표현력 양성을 목적으로 하는 영어 문장 재현 연습용의 교재는 다음과 같은 요건을 갖춘 것이 가장 효과가 높다는 것입니다.

첫째 교재 본문의 내용이 학습자의 지속적인 흥미와 관심을 끌 수 있을 만큼 재미 있으면서도 교육적 가치가 풍부한 것이어야 하며,

둘째 교재에 사용되는 단어, 숙어, 문법구조등이 각 학습단계(입문, 초급, 중급, 상급수준 등)에 꼭 알맞게 제한 사용되어야 하며,

셋째 재현 연습에 쓰일 본문의 길이도 기억과 재현에 알맞는 단어수(학습 단계에 따라 150 단어 내지 350 단어의 길이)를 초과하지 않아야 하고,

넷째 학습시키고자 하는 단어, 숙어, 문법구조등이 교재의 본문에 흡수·통합되어 이것들이 각기 따로 따로 유리되어 있을 때보다 높은 차원의 「의미내용」을 갖도록 하여야 한다는 것입니다.

따라서 영어의 표현력과 이해력의 종합적인 향상을 위해서는 무엇보다 먼저 위에 열거한 네가지 요건을 갖춘 교재가 절대 필요한 것입니다. 그런데 이러한 교재의 입수가 지극히 어렵던 차에, 다행히 옥스포드대학출판부에서, 이 방면의 세계적 권위자인 L.A.HILL 박사로 하여금 위에 적은 네가지 요건을 모두 갖춘 영어 학습교재 총서를 저술케하여, 이를 최근에 모두 펴 내놓아 외국어로서 영어를 배우는 전세계 영어학도들의 절

찬을 받고 있는 것을 보고, 실용 영어의 통신교육과 그에 부수되는 영어 교재의 출판을 전문으로 하고 있는 저희 外國語研修社에서는, 이 교재의 한국내 출판이 저희들의 사업목적에 부합될 뿐 아니라 이러한 교재를 찾고 있는 수 많은 독자와 영어 교사들에게 크게 도움이 되리라고 생각하고 작년부터 옥스포드대학출판부와 판권 교섭을 해 오던 끝에 금년들어 계약이 성립되어 **L. A. HILL**박사 저술의 영어 학습 교재중 **표현력** 및 이해력 향상에 역점을 둔 교재 전 **4**집을 아래와 같이 내놓게 되었읍니다.

제 1 집 **Stories for Reproduction 1**: 입문편, 초급편, 중급편 및 상급편의 Text 각 1 권과 그 Study Guide(학습안내서)각 1 권 및 이에 딸린 음성교재용 녹음테이프.

제 2 집 **Stories for Reproduction 2**: 입문편, 초급편, 중급편 및 상급편의 Text 각 1 권과 그 Answer Key 각 1 권 및 이에 딸린 음성교재용 녹음테이프.

제 3 집 **Steps to Understanding**: 입문편, 초급편, 중급편 및 상급편의 Text 각 1 권과 그 Answer Key 각 1 권 및 이에 딸린 음성교재용 녹음테이프.

제 4 집 **Stories for Reproduction (American Series)**: 초급편, 중급편 및 상급편의 Text 각 1 권과 그 **Answer Key** 및 이에 딸린 음성교재용 녹음테이프.

전 세계적인 Best Seller 가 되어 있는 이 교재는 표현력과 독해력 향상에 필수적인 단어·숙어와 문법구조를 4 단계로 나누어 제한 사용하고 있어 독자들에게 학습상의 부담을 주지 않을 뿐 아니라 그 본문이 유우머(해학)와 윗트(기지)로 가득찬 흥미진진한 짧은 이야기로 되어 있기 때문에 그것을 끝까지 단숨에 읽을 수 있도록 되어 있으며, 이 이야기를 속독, 청취, 정독, 재청(再聽)한 다음 다양한 **Questions**와 **Exercises** 를 사용한 문답식 방법으로 그 내용을 이해하는 훈련을 쌓는 동시에 이를 다시 말과 글로 표현해 보는(**Oral & Written Reproduction**)연습을 되풀이 함으로써, 난해한 영문국역, 단편적인 단어·숙어의 암기나 문법체계의 학습등에서 오는 정신적 긴장과 피로를 수반하지 않고, 독자들이 이야기의 내용을 즐기다 보면 자기도 모르는 사이에 이해력과 표현력이 몸에 붙도록 꾸며져 있읍니다.

또한 이 교재는 Text와는 따로 **Study Guide**(학습안내서), **Answer Key** (해답집) 및 녹음테이프가 딸려 있어 개인의 자습(Self-Study)용으로는 물론 교실 수업용으로도 쓸 수 있도록 만들어져 있읍니다.

이 교재가 많은 독자들의 영어 표현력 및 이해력 향상에 획기적인 도움이 되기를 바랍니다.

1985년 1월 5일

外國語研修社

代表理事
會 長 李 瀅 載

머 리 말

이 책은 Stories for Reproduction Series(이야기의 재현을 통하여 배우는 영어 총서)
제4집에 해당되는 American Series(미국영어판 전3권)의 셋째권(상급편)으로서 영
어를 제2차어 또는 외국어로서 배우는 학생들을 위하여 쓰여진 것입니다. 이 책은 미국
영어(American English)를 문맥적으로 읽고 이해하는 연습을 시키는 것을 목적으로 만
들어진 것이며, 약 150단어 길이로 쓰여진 익살스러운 이야기 30편을 담고 있습니다.
각편의 이야기마다 독해문제(Reading Comprehension Questions)들과 2개의 어휘연
습(Vocabulary Exercises) 문제들이 뒤따르고 있습니다.

이야기와 연습문제는 L. A. Hill박사의 2,075 표제어 수준으로 쓰여진 것입니다. 이
책 62-70 페이지의 부록A 에 이 2,075단어 어휘가 전부 수록되어 있습니다. 가끔 이
2,075단어 수준을 초과하는 단어가 하나 또는 그 이상 이야기 속에 나오는데 이 경우에
는 이야기 끝에 열거하고 Outside the 2,075 Words(2,075 단어 범위외)라고 표시해 두
었읍니다. 선생님은 이 단어들을 수업중에 설명해 주거나 학생들로 하여금 이야기를 읽기
전에 사전에서 그 뜻을 찾아 보도록 하는 것이 좋겠읍니다. 연습문제는 지시어로서 특
수어가 사용되고 있으므로, 이 특수어가 쓰여진 연습문제의 문맥에 따라 이 단어들의
의미를 학생들에게 알려주어야 할 것입니다.

이 책에 쓰여진 문법구조도 또한 용의주도하게 통제되어 있읍니다. 문법체계에 대한
설명은 71페이지에 있는 부록B 에 있읍니다.

이 책을 이용하는 방법

교실수업에서 이 책을 이용하는 경우에는 이 책의 이야기(Stories)와 연습문제(Exercises)
를 청해(聽解 – Listening Comprehension) 및 독해(讀解 – Reading Comprehension) 연습
의 일부로 이용할 수 있으며, 또한 말하기(Speaking) 및 쓰기(Writing)의 생산적 기능
(Productive Skills)을 연마하는데 이용할 수도 있읍니다.

독자적으로 공부하는 학생들에게는 이야기(Stories)가 독해(讀解)와 필기재현(筆記
再現 – Written Reproduction) 용으로 꼭 알맞을 것입니다.

교실수업의 경우

선생님은 이 이야기들을 학생들의 「듣고 이해하기(Aural Comprehension)」와 문어
체 영어(Written English)」의 이해를 향상시키기 위해 이용할 수 있을 것입니다.

먼저 선생님이 이야기를 2~3회 낭독하되 학생들로 하여금 책을 덮고 듣게 합니다. 그 다음에는 학생들에게 이 이야기를 구두 또는 필기로, 자신의 말을 써서 다시 이야기로 엮어 보도록 하거나 내용파악문제(Comprehension Questions)에 답을 제공함으로써 이야기의 줄거리를 재표현해 보도록 합니다.

내용파악문제는 이야기를 읽힌 다음 구두연습의 일부로서 대답하도록 하거나, 이야기를 들려주었을 경우에 청취해야 할 요점들을 미리 검토해 보도록 하기 위하여 이야기를 읽히기 전에 제시해 주어도 무방합니다. 그러면 학생들은 이야기가 낭독될 때 구두나 필기로 그 해답을 제공할 수 있을 것입니다.

해답을 공책에 쓰게 하는 경우에는 선생님은 학생들로 하여금 한 사람씩 자신이 쓴 답을 발표하도록 함으로써 학습 효과를 높일 수 있을 것입니다. 선생님은 학생들에게 해답의 대안을 요구할 수도 있겠는데 그럴 경우에는 가끔 활발한 토론이 유발되기도 할 것입니다.

음성교재(카셋트 녹음)

이 책에는 테이프 카셋트가 딸려 있는데, 이것은 미국구어영어(Spoken American English)의 본보기로 삼을 수 있을 것입니다. 이 카셋트에는 독해용 이야기 전문과「내용파악문제」가 녹음되어 있읍니다.

가정학습의 경우

독자적으로 공부하는 학생들은「내용파악문제」를 풀거나 연습문제를 완성하기 전에 최소한 2회 이야기를 음독(音讀) 또는 묵독(黙讀)하거나 그것을 카셋트에서 들어 보는 것이 좋을 것입니다.

이야기를 듣거나 읽고 난 다음에는 그것을 기억해 낼 수 있는 최대한까지 공책에 써 보고 이야기의 원문과 대조하면서 틀린 곳을 바로잡아 나가는 것이 작문력 향상을 위하여는 무엇보다 효과적입니다.

연습문제의 완성

이야기에 따라 연습문제가 달라지나 일반적인 유형은 다음과 같읍니다.

1. 내용파악문제에 구두로 답하기
2. 적합한 단어를 넣어 공란을 채우기
3. 유사어 및 반의어 알아맞히기
4. 가로 세로 단어의 짝을 맞추기

5. 정확한 문장 고르기

6. 그림을 단어로 바꾸기

7. 그림에 맞는 문장 고르기

8. 시제(時制)의 일치

9. 이야기의 재구성

10. 읽고 이해하기(讀解)

연습문제는 교실수업의 일부로서 구두(口頭) 또는 필기(筆記)로 완성케하거나 숙제로서 내줍니다. 어느 경우에나 연습문제는 수업중에 이야기가 제시된 후 완성토록 하여야 합니다. 해답은 교사가 수업중에 검토하거나 개별적으로 점검해 줍니다.

학생들의 선택에 따라 공란에 채워 넣거나 완전한 이야기를 쓰도록 되어 있는 연습문제에 있어서는, 미국영어를 문맥에 따라 써 보는 추가 연습을 시키는 방편의 하나로서 후자를 권장합니다.

L. A. Hill박사가 2075 표제어 수준으로 쓴 교재에는 다음과 같은 것들이 있읍니다.

Word Power 4,500: Vocabulary Tests and Exercises in Amercian English.

Advanced Stories for Reproduction, Series 1.

Advanced Stories for Reproduction, Series 2.

Advanced Steps to Understanding.

Note-taking Practice.

A Fourth Crossword Puzzle Book.

Cotexturalized Vocabulary Test, Book 3.

Introduction

Advanced Stories for Reproduction is the third in a series of three readers for students of English as a Second or Foreign Language. This book is designed to give students practice in reading and understanding American English in context. *Advanced Stories for Reproduction* contains thirty humorous stories, each approximately 150 words in length. Every story is followed by reading comprehension questions and two exercises for reinforcement of vocabulary and structure.

The stories and exercises are written at Dr. L. A. Hill's 2075 word level. The complete American English word list is given in Appendix A, pages 62–70. Occasionally, one or more words that fall outside the author's list are introduced into a story. These words are listed after the story as *Outside the 2075 words*. The teacher can then explain these words in class or have the students look them up in a dictionary before reading the story.

Certain technical words are also introduced in the exercises as part of the language of directions. These words are *blank space, bracket, correct order, form, puzzle,* and *set.* Some of these words also fall outside of the author's list. In either case, the students should be informed of the meaning of these words within the context of the exercises in which they occur.

The grammatical structures used within this book have also been carefully controlled. The grammatical system is explained in Appendix B, page 71.

Suggestions for Using this Book

The stories and exercises in this book can be used as part of a whole class activity in listening and reading comprehension, and can also provide practice in the productive skills of speaking and writing. Students working independently will find the stories useful for reading comprehension and written reproduction.

In the Classroom

The teacher can use these stories to improve the students' aural comprehension and their understanding of written English.

The teacher should introduce the material by reading the story aloud, two or three times, while students listen with books closed. Students may then be asked to re-tell the passage in their own words, either orally or in writing, or they may be asked to reproduce the basic story by answering the *Comprehension Questions*.

Comprehension Questions may be answered after the reading, as an oral activity, or they may be presented prior to the reading as a preview of important points to listen for in the presentation. Students could then provide the answers orally, or in writing, when the selection has been read aloud.

If written answers are used, the teacher can provide immediate reinforcement by asking one student at a time to read his or her answer aloud to the class. The teacher can then ask the class for alternative answers, which often result in a lively discussion.

Cassette Recording

A tape cassette is available to accompany the book and may be used as a model of spoken American English. The cassette contains the complete text of the reading passages and includes the *Comprehension Questions* that accompany each reading.

At Home

For students working independently, it is suggested that they read the story to themselves, either aloud or silently, or listen to it on the cassette, at least twice before attempting to answer the *Comprehension Questions* and complete the exercises. Each student may wish to write down as much of the story as he can remember, using the original passage to check his work.

Completing the Exercises

Exercises vary from story to story but include the following general types:

1. Oral Comprehension Questions
2. Fill in the Blank Spaces
3. Synonym and Antonym Identification
4. Crossword Puzzle Completion
5. Correct Sentence Selection
6. Picture/Word Substitutions
7. Picture Identification
8. Sequencing of Events
9. Story Reconstruction
10. Reading Comprehension

Exercises may be completed orally or in writing, as part of a whole class activity or assigned as homework. In either case, exercises should be completed shortly after the story is presented in class. Answers may be checked in class or individually by the teacher.

For those exercises in which the students can either fill in the blank spaces or write out the complete story, the latter is recommended as a means of providing additional student practice in writing American English in context.

Advanced Stories for Reproduction

AMERICAN SERIES

1 Jack Hawkins was the football coach at an American college, and he was always trying to find good players, but they weren't always smart enough to be accepted by the college.

One day the coach brought an excellent young player to the dean of the college and asked that the student be allowed to enter without an examination. "Well," the dean said after some persuasion, "I'd better ask him a few questions first."

Then he turned to the student and asked him some very easy questions, but the student didn't know any of the answers.

At last the dean said, "Well, what's five times seven?"

The student thought for a long time and then answered, "Thirty-six."

The dean threw up his hands and looked at the coach in despair, but the coach said earnestly, "Oh, please let him in, sir! He was only wrong by two."

A. Answer these questions:

1. Why did the football coach want the dean to let the student enter college without an examination?
2. What question did the dean ask the student?
3. What was the student's answer?
4. What did the dean do then?

Outside the 2,075 words: coach (n.)

5. What did the coach say to the dean?
6. Who was better at arithmetic, the student or the coach?

B. Which words in the story mean the same as:

1. permitted
2. lack of hope
3. trying to get someone to agree
4. very good
5. very seriously

C. Write the sentence for each picture, choosing the correct word under each blank space.

1. 2. 3.

1. The results of all the examinations were _____.
   (confident)
   (confidential)

2. The coach was _____ that the young player would be ad-
   (confident)
   (confidential)
   mitted to the college.

3. The college was in the middle of a _____ park.
   (wooded)
   (wooden)

4. 5. 6.

4. The coach lived in a _____ house near the college.
   (wooded)
   (wooden)

5. The football player was an _____ man: he told very funny
   (imaginary)
   (imaginative)
   stories to his friends.

6. The young player often dreamed of winning _____ foot-
   (imaginary)
   (imaginative)
   ball games.

3

2 John was ten years old, and he was a very lazy boy. He had to go to school of course, but he was bored there and tried to do as little work as possible. His father and mother were both doctors and they hoped that he would become one, too, when he grew up, but one day John said to his mother, "When I finish school, I want to become a garbage collector."

"A garbage collector?" his mother asked. She was very surprised. "That's not a very pleasant job. Why do you want to become a garbage collector?"

"Because then I'd only have to work one day a week," John answered.

"Only one day a week?" his mother said. "What do you mean?"

"Well," John answered, "I know that the ones who come to our house only work on Wednesday, because I only see them on that day."

A. Answer these questions:

1. What kind of boy was John?
2. What did his parents want him to be when he grew up?
3. What did John say he wanted to be?
4. Why did John want this job?
5. How did his mother feel about this?
6. Why did John think that garbage collectors only worked one day a week?

B. Which words in the story mean the opposite of:

1. despaired
2. impossible
3. interested
4. replied
5. start
6. unpleasant

C. Put two words in each blank space in the second sentence of each pair (both sentences have the same meaning):

Example: a. When John arrived home, he told his mother his decision.
        b. <u>Arriving at</u> home, John told his mother his decision.

1. a. After John had watched the garbage collectors on his street, he decided he wanted to become one, too.
   b. _____ the garbage collectors on his street, John decided he wanted to become one, too.
2. a. Before John decided to become a garbage collector, he did not know what he wanted to be.
   b. _____ to become a garbage collector, John did not know what he wanted to be.
3. a. While John studied at school, he was bored all the time.
   b. _____ at school, John was bored all the time.
4. a. John surprised his mother because he said that he wanted to become a garbage collector.
   b. John surprised his mother _____ that he wanted to become a garbage collector.

3 Soon after Dave left college, one of his uncles, who was rich and had no children of his own, died and left Dave a lot of money, so he decided to set up his own real estate agency.

He found a nice office, bought some new furniture and moved in. He had only been there for a few hours when he heard someone coming towards the door of his office.

"It's my first customer!" he thought. He quickly picked up the telephone and pretended to be very busy answering an important call from someone in New York who wanted to buy a big and expensive house in the country.

The man knocked at the door while this was going on, came in and waited politely for the agent to finish his conversation. Then he said to him, "I'm from the telephone company, and I was sent here to connect your telephone."

A. Answer these questions:

1. How did Dave get money to set up his real estate agency?
2. What did he do to set it up?
3. What happened after he had been in his office for a few hours?

Outside the 2,075 words: customer, real estate

4. What did he think, and then do about this?
5. What did the man do?
6. And what did he say when Dave finished talking?

B. Complete this puzzle:

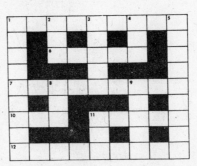

Across:
1. He's a very _____ worker: he never wastes time on the job.
6. Very big.
7. Possession.
10. The telephone man waited until the _____ of Dave's conversation before he spoke to him.
11. We often say this at the beginning of a telephone conversation.
12. Dave found a nice office _____ in town.

Down:
1. The man who came to Dave's office was one of the _____ of the telephone company.
2. When there is a _____ at sea, you can't see very far.
3. People _____ when their team scores a goal.
4. Put into one's mouth, chew and swallow.
5. The man came to Dave's office to connect the _____ .
8. Move your head to show that you mean *yes*.
9. Divide into two equal parts.
11. "_____ can you use the telephone when it hasn't been connected?" "You can't."

C. Write this story, using words instead of the pictures:

Before he could open his office, Dave had to buy a lot of things to furnish it. For the hall, he bought a nice , and for his own office, with comfortable , a pretty for his desk light, and a red

Unfortunately, the telephone people had to make holes in some of the walls with an electric , after which another man had to come to and the walls again.

7

4 Mr. Smith lived in the country, but he worked in an office in the big city, so five days a week he went to work by train every morning and came home the same way.

One morning he was reading his newspaper on the train when a man sitting behind him, who Mr. Smith had never met before, leaned forward, tapped him on the shoulder and spoke to him. The man said, "You're not leading a very interesting life, are you? You get on the same train at the same station at the same time every morning, and you always sit in the same seat and read the same newspaper."

Mr. Smith put his paper down, turned around, and said to the man angrily, "How do you know all that about me?"

"Because I'm always sitting in this seat behind you," the man answered.

A. Answer these questions:

1. How did Mr. Smith go to and from his office every day?
2. What happened to him on the train one morning?
3. What was he doing when this happened?
4. What did the man say to Mr. Smith?
5. What did Mr. Smith ask the man?
6. Why did the man know so much about him?

B. Which of these sentences are true? Write down the correct ones.

1. Mr. Smith did not go to his office on weekends.
2. Mr. Smith went to his office by train five days a week.
3. While he was reading his newspaper one day, he leaned forward and tapped a man on the shoulder.
4. While he was reading his newspaper one day, he was tapped on the shoulder by another man.
5. The man sitting behind him had never seen Mr. Smith before.
6. The man sitting behind Mr. Smith always saw him in the same seat.
7. The man thought Mr. Smith's life was dull.
8. The man thought Mr. Smith's life was very interesting.
9. The man's own life was much more interesting than Mr. Smith's.
10. The man's own life was just as uninteresting as Mr. Smith's.

C. Write the number of the correct sentence under each picture:

1. He always sat in the same seat every day.
2. He got on the train.
3. He hurried to the train station.
4. He read his newspaper thoroughly.
5. He turned around and spoke angrily to the man who had interrupted his reading.
6. Mr. Smith put his newspaper down.
7. Mr. Smith left his house at 7:00 A.M. every morning.
8. One day another passenger tapped him on the shoulder.

9

5 Lisa was an attractive young woman, and she always combed her hair neatly and wore pretty clothes. She worked in a small town and earned enough money to take a vacation in the mountains during the summer.

The first time that Lisa went there, she discovered that she hadn't brought enough money. At first she was worried, but then she remembered that she had brought her checkbook with her and went to the bank to cash a check. The bank teller had never seen Lisa before, but he knew that a lot of people were stealing checkbooks and using them, so he said to her, "Can you identify yourself, please?"

Lisa had never been asked to do this in her home town, so she looked puzzled for a moment; but then she took her mirror out of her handbag, looked at it, and then said happily, "Yes, it *is* me."

Outside the 2075 words: cash (v.), identify

A. Answer these questions:

1. Where did Lisa go for her vacation?
2. Why did she have to go to the bank during her vacation?
3. What did the bank teller ask her?
4. Why did he say this?
5. How did Lisa feel about this?
6. What did she do and then say?

B. Which of these answers are correct? Write down the questions and the correct answers.

1. Was Lisa an attractive woman?
   a. Yes, she was.
   b. No, she wasn't.
2. Could she afford to take a summer vacation?
   a. Yes, she could.
   b. No, she couldn't.
3. What worried her on her first vacation in the mountains?
   a. She didn't have enough money.
   b. She had forgotten her checkbook.
4. Why didn't the bank teller want to cash her check?
   a. Because he had never seen her before.
   b. Because he knew that she had stolen the checkbook.
5. What did the bank teller ask her to do?
   a. To make sure that she was really Lisa.
   b. To show him some proof that she was Lisa.
6. What did Lisa do to identify herself?
   a. She looked in her mirror.
   b. She showed the bank teller a photograph of herself.

C. Write this story, putting one word in each blank space. You will find all the correct words in the story on page 10.

George worked in a bank as a _____. One day an _____ young woman came into the bank and gave him a _____. She wanted him to _____ it for her, but George had never seen her before, so he said, "Can you _____ yourself?"

The woman was very _____ when she heard this. She was on _____ from her home town, and hadn't brought much money. But then she opened her _____, took out a photograph of herself, and showed it to George, smiling _____.

George looked at it for a _____ and then said, "Yes, that's you," and he gave her the money.

11

6 A large store was having its spring sale on shoes and boots. It was the first day of the sale, and the shoe department was full of women who were eagerly trying to buy them. There were all kinds of shoes and boots in a variety of colors, and the prices had been reduced a lot, because the store wanted to get rid of as many as possible in order to make room for their new stock.

The cashiers were kept busy, and at one moment a woman came to one of them with her money in her hand and said, "I don't need a bag, thank you. I'm wearing the shoes I bought." She pointed to them on her feet.

"Would you like a bag to put your *old* shoes in then?" the cashier asked politely as she took the woman's money.

"No, thank you," the woman answered quickly, "I've just sold those to someone else."

A. Answer these questions:

1. What were on sale in the large store that week?
2. Why were they being sold cheaply?
3. Was the sale successful?
4. What did a woman say to one of the cashiers?
5. What did the cashier ask her?
6. Why didn't the woman need a bag?

Outside the 2,075 words: cashier

12

B. Write the sentence for each picture, choosing the correct word under each blank space.

1.  2.  3.

1. This woman has been to a lot of sales _____ .
(late)
(lately)

2. She never gets to a sale _____ : she is always one of the first to arrive.
(late)
(lately)

3. She is _____ sure that she will find some shoes she likes.
(prettily)
(pretty)

4.  5.  6.

4. She doesn't want to get her size _____ .
(wrong)
(wrongly)

5. She wants to make _____ sure of the size by asking.
(double)
(doubly)

6. She is examining the heels _____ now.
(close)
(closely)

C. Draw lines from the words on the left to the correct words on the right. Then write out the five complete sentences.

1. The cashier
2. Another woman
3. The woman
4. The shoes and boots
5. The store

a. had bought the woman's old shoes.
b. had sold her old shoes.
c. offered the woman a bag.
d. was having a sale.
e. were of all kinds and colors.

7 Fred had a very rusty old car, but his father said that he had to sell
it before he would buy him a new one.

"You have to learn the value of money, Fred," his father said.
"It doesn't grow on trees, you know. You should learn to be a
good businessman."

But nobody seemed to want to buy the car from Fred. He put a
"For Sale" sign in the back window of the car, and he put another
sign on the bulletin board in his college dormitory, but nothing
happened. Then one day he was driving to another town, and
stopped at the entrance to a toll booth where he had to pay before
being allowed to use the road.

The attendant said, "Two dollars and fifty cents."

"I accept," said Fred. "It's yours." Then he put the car keys into
the surprised attendant's hand, and held out his other hand for
the two dollars and fifty cents.

Outside the 2,075 words: toll booth

14

A. Answer these questions:

1. When would Fred's father buy him a new car?
2. How did Fred try to sell his car?
3. Why did Fred stop at a toll booth?
4. What did the attendant say to Fred?
5. What did Fred say and then do to the attendant?
6. Did the attendant want to buy Fred's car?

B. Which words in the story mean the same as:

1. to receive willingly
2. astonished
3. permitted
4. way in
5. worth

C. Write this story, putting *it, where* or *which* in each blank space, but *only* if one of these words is necessary.

Fred had an old car _____ was very rusty. He wanted to sell _____ .
                (1)   (2)

He didn't care _____ what price he got for _____ . He tried to sell _____
                  (3)   (4)   (5)

by putting up a notice in the dormitory of the college _____ he was
                                         (6)

studying, but _____ was no use. One of the difficulties _____ Fred
        (7)   (8)

faced was that all the other students had better cars than his. But there

was a place on the way to the next town _____ there was a toll booth,
                                    (9)

and Fred even drove his old car there and tried to get the attendant

to buy _____ .
  (10)

8 A traveling salesman had to walk so much that his feet often hurt. His doctor told him that salt water was the best thing for them, so the salesman decided to go to the sea for his vacation that year. Since all of the hotels near the sea were expensive, he went to a small hotel far away from the beach.

In the morning he went down to the calm sea with a bucket, went over to the lifeguard and asked whether he would be allowed to take a bucket of salt water. The lifeguard seemed very surprised but said, "Yes, although you'll have to pay twenty-five cents for it."

The salesman gave the lifeguard twenty-five cents, filled his bucket, took it to his hotel and put his feet in the water.

After lunch, he came down to the beach again. The tide had gone out now, so the sea was much lower. The salesman thought, "That man has a very good business. He must have sold thousands of buckets since this morning."

Outside the 2,075 words: lifeguard

A. Answer these questions:

1. Why did the salesman's feet hurt?
2. Why did the salesman go to the sea for his vacation?
3. What did he ask the lifeguard?
4. What did the lifeguard say to the salesman?
5. What did the salesman do then?
6. Why was the sea much lower in the afternoon?
7. What did the salesman think?

B. Which words in the story mean the opposite of:

1. cheap
2. forbidden
3. close to
4. higher
5. rough

C. Complete the second sentence in each pair (both sentences have the same meaning):

Example: a. The salesman had difficulty in finding an inexpensive hotel.
   b. It was difficult <u>for the salesman to find an inexpensive hotel.</u>

1. a. Frequently, doctors used to send their patients to the seashore for a rest.
   b. It was very common _____.

2. a. The salesman behaved stupidly when he asked the lifeguard whether he could take some water.
   b. It was stupid _____.

3. a. The lifeguard was able to cheat the salesman easily.
   b. It was easy _____.

4. a. The salesman was being silly when he thought the lifeguard had sold thousands of buckets of water.
   b. It was silly _____.
5. a. Nobody could possibly know so little.
   b. It would be impossible _____.

9 An important businessman was asked to give a twenty-minute speech in another city. He was too busy to write it himself, so he asked his secretary to put one together for him out of a large book of speeches which she had on her desk. She typed one out for him, and he picked it up just in time to rush off to his plane. But when he gave his speech, it ran on for an hour, and the audience was getting very restless and bored by the end of it.

When the businessman got back to his office, he complained to his secretary about this. "I told you it was supposed to be a twenty-minute speech!" he said to her bitterly.

"That's what I gave you," she answered, "the original and two copies. The original for you to read at the meeting, and two copies for the files, after you had checked them."

A. Answer these questions:

1. What was the important businessman asked to do?
2. Who prepared the speech for him?
3. How did the audience receive it?
4. Why did the speech last an hour instead of twenty minutes?
5. Why had the secretary given him so many copies?
6. What mistake had the businessman made?

Outside the 2,075 words: file (n.)

B. Complete this puzzle:

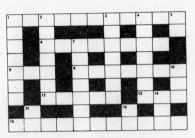

Across:

1. The _____ in this story had to give a speech.
6. When he was sick, he used to take some _____ .
8. "Did the man only read one copy of his speech?"
   "No, he read _____ three of them."
9. The businessman's plane is _____ now.

12. Travel by plane, instead of by train, _____ time.
13. The businessman should _____ have read more than one copy of his speech.
16. The businessman's audience did not find his speech very _____ after the first time.

Down:

1.

2. The businessman always took _____ of his company's prod-

ucts with him to show other people.
3. There are sixty in a minute.
4. The secretary forgot to _____ that there were two extra copies of the speech when she gave them to her employer.
5. The businessman had _____ time to write his own speeches.
7. The businessman had to _____ his speech in another city.
10. The businessman _____ his secretary to type his speech.
11. The businessman was met _____ arrival at the airport.
14. "Did the businessman have his _____ plane?"
    "No, he flew with the commercial airlines."
15. The businessman had to read his speech _____ the meeting.

C. Write this story, using words instead of the pictures:

Before the businessman's there was a party for him to

meet members of the To drink, there was

red and white _____ , and a big glass _____ with a

mixture of orange and _____ juice in it. To eat, there were

small _____ which tasted of _____

10 A young man was called up for army service, but he didn't want to become a soldier. When he went for his medical exam, he pretended that his eyesight was very bad.

The doctor pointed to the eye chart on the wall and said, "Please read the top line."

"The top line of what?" the young man asked.

"The top line of the chart," the doctor replied.

"What chart?" the man asked.

"The one on the wall," the doctor said.

"What wall?" the man asked.

Finally, the doctor decided that the man's eyes were not good enough for army service.

That evening the same young man was at a movie when another man came in and sat next to him in the dark. When the lights went on, the young man saw that his neighbor was the doctor who had examined him earlier. Immediately he said, "Excuse me, ma'am, but does this bus go to Main Street?"

A. Answer these questions:

1. What did the young man do to avoid military service?
2. What did he say when the doctor said, "Please read the top line of the chart"?
3. What did the doctor decide at last?

Outside the 2,075 words: chart

20

4. Where did the **young man** go that evening?
5. Who sat down **next** to him?
6. What did the young man say when the lights went on?

B. Which of these sentences are true? Write down the correct ones.

1. The young man in this story was unwilling to do his military service.
2. The young man in this story was willing to do his military service.
3. He avoided it by pretending that he had bad eyesight.
4. He failed to get in because his eyesight was very bad.
5. When the doctor gave him orders, he could not understand what the doctor said.
6. When the doctor told him to look at things, he pretended he could not see them.
7. He went into a movie theater by mistake, thinking it was a bus.
8. He went into a movie theater to see a film.
9. The doctor came into the theater with the young man.
10. The doctor came into the theater after the young man.

C. Write the number of the correct sentence under each picture:

1. He asked him whether the bus he was on went to Main Street.
2. He went to the doctor for a medical exam.
3. Someone came in and sat down next to him in the dark.
4. The doctor tested his eyes.
5. Then he let the young man go.
6. A young man got a letter from the army.
7. The young man went to a movie that evening.
8. When the lights came on, the young man saw that it was the doctor.

11 A young officer on a small vessel was being tested on his knowledge of what to do if someone fell overboard while he was in charge of the ship. A big can was thrown into the sea, and the officer had to pretend it was a man who had fallen in and try to save it. The officer was inexperienced, and the first thing that happened was that the can was pulled under by the ship's propeller. The officer quickly stopped the ship and went backwards. There was a loud crash as he struck the can again. Then he went forwards, went around in a circle, and struck the can once more straight in front of the ship.

A sailor who was observing all this now said, "Excuse me, sir, but if I'm ever unfortunate enough to fall into the sea while you're steering the ship, please let me swim to shore by myself!"

Outside the 2,075 words: propeller

A. Answer these questions:

1. What was the young officer being tested on?
2. How was he being tested?
3. What was the first thing that happened?
4. What did the officer do then?
5. What happened when he went forwards?
6. What did a sailor say to him then?

B. Which of these answers are correct? Write down the questions and the correct answers.

1. What kind of test was the young officer having?
   a. It was a test of whether he could save a person who fell into the sea.
   b. It was a test of whether he was in charge of the ship.
2. What did the officer have to save in the test?
   a. A man who had fallen into the sea.
   b. A can which had been thrown into the sea.
3. What did the propeller do to the can?
   a. It made it go around.
   b. It pulled it under the water.
4. How did the officer hit the can the second time?
   a. He hit it when he had stopped.
   b. He hit it while he was going backwards.
5. How did he hit it the third time?
   a. He went around and hit it with the front of the ship.
   b. He put it in a circle and hit it with the back of the ship.
6. What did a sailor want the officer to do?
   a. To let him swim to shore if he ever fell into the sea.
   b. To save him if he ever fell into the sea.

C. Write this story, putting one word in each blank space. You will find all the correct words in the story on page 22.

The captain of a small _____ went below deck to sleep, leaving a young officer in _____ of the ship. This young man did not have much _____ about _____ a ship yet, and he was too _____ to avoid hitting a large rock. The ship _____ it twice. The _____ woke the captain, and he _____ put on his clothes and hurried onto the deck.

He stood for a few seconds, _____ the scene and then said, "Well, you said you'd never been in a shipwreck before: now you're in one."

23

12 When George Jones finished college, he became a clerk in a big company, hoping to advance to higher positions as time went on. He did his work reasonably well, but he wasn't very smart, so when the older employees retired from higher positions, it was never Jones who was promoted.

After he had been with the company for fifteen years without ever being promoted, a smart young man, straight from college, came to work in the same department, and after a year, he was promoted above Jones.

Jones was angry that he hadn't been promoted instead of this young man, so he went to his manager and said, "I've had sixteen years' experience on this job, yet a new man has been promoted over my head after having been here only one year."

"I'm sorry, Jones," answered the manager patiently, "but you haven't had sixteen years' experience: you've had one year's experience sixteen times."

A. Answer these questions:

1. What job did George Jones get after leaving college?
2. What was his ambition?
3. Why didn't he get promoted?

Outside the 2,075 words: promote

4. Who joined the same department fifteen years after him?
5. What happened after a year?
6. Why did Jones go to see the manager?
7. What did Jones say to him?
8. What did the manager answer?

B. Write these sentences, choosing the correct word under each blank space.

1. The man _____ above Jones's head was very _____
              (promoted)   (interested)
              (promoting)   (interesting)
in getting ahead in life.
2. The other people _____ in Jones's department found him
                           (worked)
                           (working)
_____ to talk to.
  (interested)
  (interesting)
3. Students _____ college in the summer were usually _____
             (finished)   (choosing)
             (finishing)   (chosen)
by the company in the autumn.
4. Clerks _____ to be _____ were usually young rather
          (choosing)   (promoted)
          (chosen)   (promoting)
than old.
5. The manager _____ to Jones did not think Jones was very
             (talked)
             (talking)

_____ .

  (experienced)
  (experiencing)

C. Draw lines from the words on the left to the correct words on the right. Then write out the five complete sentences.

1. Jones
2. Jones's experience
3. Older employees
4. The manager
5. The new young man

a. did not think Jones had a lot of experience.
b. retired from the company.
c. was angry because he was not promoted.
d. was promoted after a year.
e. was the same each year.

25

13 Mr. Johnson had never been up in an airplane before and he had read a lot about air accidents, so one day when a friend offered to take him for a ride in his own small plane, Mr. Johnson was very worried about accepting. Finally, however, his friend persuaded him that it was very safe, and Mr. Johnson boarded the plane.

His friend started the engine and began to taxi onto the runway of the airport. Mr. Johnson had heard that the most dangerous parts of a flight were the take-off and the landing, so he was extremely frightened and closed his eyes.

After a minute or two he opened them again, looked out of the window of the plane, and said to his friend, "Look at those people down there. They look as small as ants, don't they?"

"Those are ants," answered his friend. "We're still on the ground."

A. Answer these questions:

1. Why was Mr. Johnson worried about accepting his friend's offer to ride in his small plane?
2. What did Mr. Johnson think were the most dangerous parts of a flight?
3. How did he feel when they began to taxi onto the runway, and what did he do?
4. What happened after a minute or two?

Outside the 2,075 words: runway, take-off, taxi (v.)

5. What did Mr. Johnson say to his friend?
6. And what did the friend answer?

B. Which words in the story mean the same as:

1. afraid
2. at last
3. coming down
4. go(ing) up

5. nervous
6. entered
7. shut
8. without danger

C. Write the sentence for each picture, choosing the correct word under each blank space.

1.

2.

3.

1. Mr. Johnson has _____ his plane!
   (missed)
   (spared)

2. Mr. Johnson wants to borrow his friend's car, but the friend can't
   _____ it today.
   (miss)
   (spare)

3. Mr. Johnson is _____ a bridge.
   (crossing)
   (passing)

4.

5.

6.

4. He is _____ another bridge now.
   (crossing)
   (passing)

5. Mr. Johnson doesn't have a car today, so he'll just have to _____ one.
   (borrow)
   (lend)

6. His neighbor owns two cars. He can _____ one to Mr. Johnson.
   (borrow)
   (lend)

14 A man got into a train and found himself sitting opposite a woman who seemed to be about thirty-five years old. Soon they began talking to each other, and he said to her, "Do you have a family?"

"Yes, I have one son," the woman answered.

"Oh, really?" said the man. "Does he smoke?"

"No, he's never touched a cigarette," the woman replied.

"That's good," the man continued. "I don't smoke either. Tobacco is very bad for one's health. And does your son drink wine?"

"Oh, no," the woman answered at once, "he's never drunk a drop of it."

"Then I congratulate you, ma'am," the man said. "And does he ever come home late at night?"

"No, never," his neighbor answered. "He goes to bed immediately after dinner every night."

"Well," the man said, "he's a wise young man. How old is he?"

"He's six months old today," the woman replied proudly.

A. Answer these questions:

1. Did the woman on the train have a family?
2. What three things did the man ask her about her son?
3. What did she answer to all three questions?
4. What did the man think about her answers?
5. What was his last question?
6. And what was her answer?
7. How old do you think the man had expected the woman's son to be?

B. Which words in the story mean the opposite of:

1. a long time
2. next to
3. foolish
4. in an ashamed way
5. pity

C. Complete the second sentence in each pair (both sentences have the same meaning):

Example: a. The man found a woman sitting opposite him on the train, but he wasn't expecting to.

      b. The man wasn't expecting <u>to find a woman sitting opposite him,</u> but he did.

1. a. The woman was questioned about her son, but she hadn't been expecting this.
   b. The woman hadn't been expecting to _____ , but she was.
2. a. The man had an interesting trip, although he had not expected one.
   b. The man had not expected _____ , but he did.
3. a. The woman's son was only six months old, but the man wasn't expecting him to be so young.
   b. The man wasn't expecting the woman's son _____ , but he was.
4. a. The woman was able to speak proudly of her son, but she had not expected to on a train.
   b. The woman had not expected to _____ , but she was.

15 It was a Saturday evening in late July, and Joe and his girlfriend had been to the movies. After that they ate supper in a small restaurant, and now they were sitting together on a bench in the park, enjoying the cool air and the moonlight.

After a long time, the girl said dreamily, "Joe, do you think my eyes are like bright stars shining in the clear night sky?"

Joe looked at her quickly, and then answered, "Yes."

"And do you think my teeth are like pearls reflecting the light of the moon?" she continued in the same dreamy voice.

"Yes," he answered again after another quick look.

"And do you think my hair is like a golden waterfall in the moonlight?" she went on.

"Yes," he repeated.

"Oh, Joe!" she said happily, throwing her arms around him, "You say the most wonderful things!"

A. Answer these questions:

1. Where were Joe and his girlfriend when she began asking him these questions?
2. What was the weather like?

3. What were the girl's eyes like?
4. What were her teeth like?
5. What was her hair like?
6. Did Joe agree with these comparisons?
7. What did his girlfriend say finally?
8. Who had really been saying all those wonderful things?

B. Complete this puzzle:

Across:

1. Joe's girlfriend thought that he said _____ things.
4. Objects which are very valuable.
6. To know something when one sees it again.
9. Joe did not really seem to have the _____ to say much.
10. Joe _____ his girlfriend into the park by the hand, because it was dark.
11. Joe and his girlfriend were _____ to go home after sitting in the park.

Down:

1. The girl's hair was like a golden _____ .

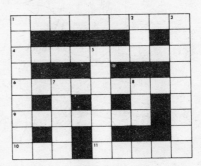

2. Joe and his girlfriend went _____ a walk after supper.
3. Joe was just _____ to what his girlfriend said, and then answering, "Yes."
5. Adding one's signature to.
7. Small girl or boy.
8. Freezing cold.

C. Write this letter, putting one of the words below in each blank space:

moonlight   blades   berries   waterfall   beam
horizon   lightning   hay   stream   rainbow

Dear Martha,

Last week the farmer in the next village cut his grass to make _____ for his cows, and Joe and I walked through it to reach the little _____ . We sat among the _____ of tall grass and ate _____ off the bushes. There was the rushing sound of a _____ near us, and when we went to look for it, we saw a colorful _____ in the sky, and flashes of _____ out near the _____ . We stayed until it got dark, and then ate our supper by the water, where a _____ of _____ shone down through the trees.

Your friend,
Sue

31

16 Mr. Grey was a biology professor, and he had a big collection of extremely rare bones which he was very proud of. Then one year he managed to get a new and better job at another university. Because Mr. Grey was very busy, his wife made the arrangements for all their possessions to be taken in a moving van to their new home while he was away at work.

The following week three men started taking the things out of Mrs. Grey's house and loading them into the van, when one of them brought out a large wooden box. He was just about to throw it into the van with all the other things when Mrs. Grey ran out of her house and said, "Please treat that box very gently! That one has all of my husband's bones in it."

The man was so surprised that he nearly dropped the box on his feet.

A. Answer these questions:

1. What kind of collection did Mr. Grey have?
2. What happened to Mr. Grey one year?
3. Why did some men come to take all of the Grey's possessions away?
4. What did one of the men take out of the house?
5. What was he going to do with the box?
6. What did Mrs. Grey say to the man?
7. What happened to the man when he heard this?

Outside the 2,075 words: biology

32

B. Which of these sentences are true? Write down the correct ones.

1. Mr. Grey had collected some bones which were very common.
2. Mr. Grey had collected a lot of bones which were very unusual.
3. He had to move to another town because he was very busy.
4. He had to move to another town because he was going to work there.
5. Mrs. Grey watched three men while they took things out of her house and loaded them into a van.
6. Three men watched Mrs. Grey while she took things out of her house and loaded them into a van.
7. Mr. Grey's collection of bones were in a large wooden box.
8. Mrs. Grey kept her dead husband's bones in a large wooden box.
9. The man who was carrying the box was very surprised when Mrs. Grey said it contained her husband's bones.
10. The man who was carrying the box was very surprised when Mrs. Grey dropped the box on his feet.

C. Write the number of the correct sentence under each picture:

1. A moving van came to the door of Mr. Grey's house.
2. He was busy at his office.
3. He was going to throw it into the van.
4. Mrs. Grey watched while the men loaded the van.
5. Mr. Grey collected a lot of rare bones.
6. Mrs. Grey stopped him, saying it contained her husband's bones.
7. One of the men brought a big wooden box out of the house.
8. The man nearly dropped it on his feet.

17 A rich young man decided that he would like to do some diving in the sea, so he bought a rubber suit and all the other things that he needed, and took some lessons at a diving school. Then one day he walked into the water by himself and began to explore the bottom of the sea.

He saw a lot of beautiful fish and other things, and then, after half an hour, he suddenly saw a man waving his arms and legs around wildly near the bottom of the sea. He was wearing only a bathing suit.

The rich young man was very surprised to see him, so he took out a plastic notebook and a special pencil, which could write under water, and wrote, "What are you doing here?"

He showed the notebook to the other man, who then took the pencil and wrote, "Drowning!"

Outside the 2,075 words: plastic

A. Answer these questions:

1. What did the rich young man want to do?
2. How did he prepare himself for this?
3. What did he first see at the bottom of the ocean?
4. What did he see later?
5. What was the man doing?
6. What was he wearing?
7. What did the rich young man do?
8. What did the other man write in the notebook?

B. Write these sentences, choosing the correct word under each blank space.

1. The teacher _____ the diving lessons was very _____ .
   (given)   (experienced)
   (giving)   (experiencing)

2. The young man being _____ the _____ lessons was rich.
   (given)   (dived)
   (giving)   (diving)

3. The fish _____ at the bottom of the sea were beautiful and _____
   (seeing)   (interested)
   (seen)   (interesting
   to look at.

4. The man _____ his arms wildly was _____ .
   (waved)   (drowned)
   (waving)   (drowning)

5. The pencil _____ specially for _____ under water was very useful.
   (made)   (writing)
   (making)   (written)

C. Draw lines from the words on the left to the correct words on the right. Then write out the five complete sentences.

1. The bottom of the sea
2. The diving school
3. The man at the bottom of the sea
4. The rich young man
5. The special pencil

a. could write under water.
b. liked exploring the bottom of the sea.
c. gave the rich young man lessons.
d. was drowning.
e. was full of beautiful fish.

35

18 Mr. Scott thought that he was very good at fixing household appliances when they broke, so when Mrs. Scott told him that she needed a new vacuum cleaner, he said, "What's wrong with the old one? I can easily fix it."

Mr. Scott fixed the vacuum cleaner, but the same thing happened again several times, until one day, after he had unscrewed all the parts, and had gone to have lunch, Mrs. Scott added a few extra pieces to the pile on the floor.

"Do you know," she said to her friend, Mrs. Brown, the next morning, "if I'd just taken away a few pieces, he'd have noticed that they were missing, and would have gone out and bought some more. But when he couldn't find places for all the pieces that were on the floor, he gave up and agreed to buy me a new machine."

Outside the 2,075 words: appliances, vacuum cleaner

A. Answer these questions:

1. What did Mr. Scott say when his wife asked for a new vacuum cleaner?
2. What did he do then?
3. How many times did this happen?
4. What did Mrs. Scott do one day when her husband went to have lunch?
5. What would Mr. Scott have done if some of the pieces of the vacuum cleaner were missing?
6. Why did Mr. Scott agree to buy a new machine?

B. Write these sentences, putting a form of *come, fall, get* or *go* in each blank space.

1. One day the electricity _____ very low, and Mrs. Scott's vacuum cleaner would not work properly.
2. Mr. Scott _____ angry when his wife asks him for a new vacuum cleaner.
3. When Mr. Scott is angry, he _____ for a long walk and _____ home much calmer.
4. Mrs. Scott is in bed now. For a long time she couldn't _____ comfortable.
5. Now she has _____ asleep.
6. Mrs. Scott's dreams have _____ true: her husband has agreed to buy her a new vacuum cleaner!
7. Mrs. Scott is _____ ready to go to the stores now.
8. Last week she _____ shopping for some new furniture.

C. Draw lines from the words on the left to the correct words on the right. Then write out the five complete sentences.

1. Mrs. Brown

2. Mr. Scott

3. Mrs. Scott

4. The extra pieces

5. The vacuum cleaner

a. didn't want to buy a new vacuum cleaner for his wife.
b. had been added by Mrs. Scott.
c. needed fixing on more than one occasion.
d. was a friend of Mrs. Scott's.
e. was smart enough to get a new vacuum cleaner.

19 When Mrs. Green retired from her job in a big city, she went to live in an attractive village out in the country, and began to go into the nearest town every Saturday to buy food. She tried several stores and finally chose the most convenient one and began to shop there regularly every week.

After she had visited the store several times, the cashier began to recognize her and to smile and say, "Good morning, Mrs. Brown," whenever she came to pay for the things she had bought.

At first Mrs. Green didn't mind this, but after a few weeks, she said to the cashier one Saturday, "Excuse me, but my last name's Green, not Brown." The cashier smiled cheerfully and said, "I'm sorry."

But the following week, she said to her, "Do you know, Mrs. Brown, there's another lady who comes to our store every Saturday who looks just like you."

A. Answer these questions:

1. Where did Mrs. Green go to live after her retirement?
2. Where did she buy her food?
3. How did the cashier greet her after a few weeks?
4. What did Mrs. Green say finally?
5. How did the cashier reply?
6. What did the cashier say to Mrs. Green the following week?

Outside the 2,075 words: cashier

B. Which words in the story mean the same as:

1. charming
2. closest
3. happily

4. next
5. started
6. suitable

C. Write the sentences for each picture, choosing the correct word under each blank space.

1. Soon after coming to the village, Mrs. Green became _____
   (know)
   (known)
   for her good work at the hospital.

2. She did not _____ many people
   (know)
   (known)
   there before she began working.

3. One day, Mrs. Green heard her name _____ in town.
   (mention)
   (mentioned)

4. She often heard people _____
   (discuss)
   (discussed)
   her work when she was in the city, too.

5. Although she was tired, Mrs. Green made herself _____ out
   (go)
   (gone)
   shopping.

6. She had not _____ out shopping
   (go)
   (gone)
   for the past three days.

7. Mrs. Green bought a lot of things in the store, and she wanted them _____ to her
   (deliver)
   (delivered)
   house.

8. She wanted someone _____
   (delivered)
   (to deliver)
   her things to her house every week.

20 Helen was going to have her first baby very soon. One evening it was time to take her to the hospital, so her husband, Sam, helped her get into the car and drove her there. A nurse took Helen to her room and told Sam that he could go home and she would call him when the baby arrived, but Sam said he would rather wait at the hospital. The nurse smiled and said, "There's a waiting room at the end of the hall."

Sam was walking anxiously up and down in the corridor at about midnight when the nurse came out of his wife's room and said, with a happy smile, "Which would you have preferred, a boy or a girl?"

"A girl," answered the husband. "I have an older sister, and she was always very kind to me when I was a child."

"Well," said the nurse, "It's a boy this time."

"That's all right," answered Sam cheerfully. "That was my second choice."

Outside the 2,075 words: corridor

40

A. Answer these questions:

1. Why did Sam take Helen to the hospital?
2. What did a nurse tell Sam?
3. What did Sam say to her?
4. What was Sam doing at about midnight?
5. What did the nurse ask him?
6. Why would he have preferred a girl?
7. What did the nurse say then?
8. And what did Sam answer?

B. Which words in the story mean the opposite of:

1. calmly
2. cruel
3. liked less
4. sadly
5. younger

C. Complete the second sentence in each pair (both sentences have the same meaning):

Example: a. The nurse told Sam, "I'll call you when the baby arrives."
b. The nurse said that <u>she would call Sam</u> when <u>the baby arrived.</u>

1. a. "It's time for you to go to the hospital," Sam said to Helen.
   b. "It's time you _____ ," Sam said to Helen.
2. a. "It's too bad that I don't have a more comfortable car to take you in," Sam said.
   b. "I wish I _____ ," Sam said.
3. a. "It's silly for you to worry so much!" Helen answered, laughing.
   b. "If only you _____ !" Helen answered, laughing.
4. a. Sam had said, "I prefer to have a daughter first," but actually Helen had a son.
   b. Sam _____ it if Helen _____
      a daughter first, but actually she had a son.
5. a. It's too bad that there aren't two babies, because then they would be company for each other!
   b. If there _____ , they _____ .

21 It is often very difficult these days to find someone to come and fix your television set, or your washing machine, or any other household appliance if it breaks. Everybody wants to sell you new products, but nobody wants to fix them when they stop working.

One day Mrs. Harris discovered that her bathroom faucet was leaking, so she phoned her plumber. Three days later, he arrived.

Mrs. Harris was unhappy about the delay, which had caused her a lot of trouble.

"Well, you've finally arrived!" she said to the plumber. "I called you *three days* ago."

The plumber was not at all disturbed by this. He simply took a piece of paper out of his pocket and looked at it.

"Three days ago?" he said. "That was the 21st, wasn't it? Well, I'm sorry, but I've come to the wrong place. I was looking for Mrs. Smith's house, not yours. *She* phoned me on the 20th."

A. Answer these questions:

1. What often happens these days when someone wants something fixed?
2. Why does this happen?
3. Why did Mrs. Harris phone her plumber?
4. How long did he take to come?
5. What did Mrs. Harris say to him?

Outside the 2,075 words: appliance, plumber

6. What did the plumber do when he heard this?
7. And what did he say to Mrs. Harris?

B. Complete this puzzle:

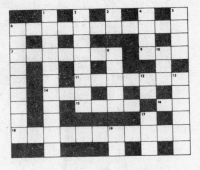

Across:

6. Television sets work by _____.
7. The hot and cold water in a bathtub comes out of _____ .
9. You can cook by electricity or by _____ .
11. A _____ came to fix Mrs. Harris's faucet.
14. The new faucet was too small, so it didn't _____ the pipe on Mrs. Harris's bathtub.
15. Mrs. Harris lived on the south _____ of the street, and Mrs. Smith lived on the north.
16. Mrs. Harris didn't phone as early _____ Mrs. Smith.
18. Mrs. Harris is _____ now.

Down:

1. Done in a very pretty or attractive way.
2. Tries.
3. Hello!
4. When Mrs. Harris heard her doorbell _____ , she hurried to open the door.
5.
6. The plumber wasted a lot of time and effort. He wasn't a very _____ worker.
8. Mrs. Harris thought she heard a _____ outside her door, so she went to see if the plumber had arrived.
10. "What do you think Mrs. Harris's _____ is?" "I think she's about thirty years old."
12. The plumber came to Mrs. Harris's house _____ car.
13. Give up one's job.
17. The plumber came to _____ Mrs. Harris's leaking faucet.
19. When Mrs. Harris turned the water _____ , the faucet leaked.

C. Write this story, putting one word in each blank space.

frames   electrician   pipe   leak
plumber   drill   faucets   plasters

Jean is very good at fixing things when they stop working around the house. When there is an electrical problem, she doesn't call the _____. She fixes it herself. When one of the _____ on the bathtub begins to _____ , she doesn't have to call the _____ . She fixes that also. She can clear a blocked _____ , and make holes for screws with her electric _____ for hanging pictures on the walls. She even _____ and paints the walls again, and _____ her own pictures.

43

22 A certain old gentleman was very unhappy about modern education, and thought that young people nowadays were not being taught the importance of knowing the difference between right and wrong.

One day he was taking a walk in the park near his home when he saw some young boys standing around a small cat. The old gentleman went up to the boys and asked them what was happening. One of the boys said to him, "We're having a contest. We're telling lies, and the one who tells the biggest one gets to keep the cat."

The old gentleman thought that this was a good opportunity to teach the boys a useful lesson, so he said to them, "I've never told a lie in my life." All at once there was a great shout from all the boys, and they said, "You've won! You can take the cat!"

A. Answer these questions:

1. How did the old gentleman feel about modern education?
2. What did he think young people should be taught?
3. What did he see in the park one day?
4. What did one of the boys tell the old gentleman?
5. What did the old gentleman think about this?
6. What did he say to the boys?
7. And what did they answer?

Outside the 2,075 words: contest

B. Which of these sentences are true? Write down the correct ones.

1. The old gentleman was not satisfied with what students were being taught.
2. The old gentleman was very satisfied with what students were being taught.
3. He wanted less attention to be paid to morals.
4. He wanted more attention to be paid to morals.
5. Some boys were having a contest for a small cat in the park.
6. Some boys were trying to sell a small cat in the park.
7. The biggest boy was going to get the cat.
8. The biggest liar was going to get the cat.
9. The old gentleman decided that he wanted the cat.
10. The old gentleman decided to teach the boys a lesson on morals.
11. The boys let him have the cat because he had told the biggest lie.
12. The boys let him have the cat because he was older than they were.

C. Write the number of the correct sentence under each picture:

1. He often got angry about what he read.
2. He said, "I've never told a lie."
3. He saw a group of boys there.
4. One day he went for a walk in the park.
5. One of the boys said, "Whoever tells the biggest lie gets to keep the cat."
6. The boys shouted, "You've won!"
7. The old gentleman read a lot about education in the newspapers.
8. When he got closer, he saw that they were standing around a small cat.

23 One day, when Mr. Smith came home from work, he found his wife very annoyed about something. Mr. Smith always thought that he was more sensible than his wife, so he started to give her a lecture on the importance of always remaining calm.

Finally he said, "It's a waste of your strength to get excited about small things. Train yourself to be patient, like me. Now, look at the fly that has just landed on my nose. Am I getting excited or annoyed? Am I swearing or waving my arms around? No, I'm not. I'm perfectly calm."

Just as he had said this, Mr. Smith started shouting. He jumped up and began to wave his arms around wildly and swear terribly. He couldn't speak for some time, but at last he was able to tell his wife: the thing on his nose hadn't been a fly, it had been a bee.

A. Answer these questions:

1. What did Mr. Smith find when he came back from work one day?
2. What did he think about himself?
3. What did he do as a result?
4. What did he say to his wife?
5. What did Mr. Smith do then?
6. Why did he do this?

B. Which of these answers are correct? Write down the questions and the correct answers.

1. How was Mrs. Smith feeling when her husband came home?
   a. She was very happy.
   b. She was very mad.
2. Why did Mr. Smith think that he could help her?
   a. Because he thought she was usually calmer than he was.
   b. Because he thought he was usually calmer than she was.
3. What did he claim to be his way of dealing with the insect on his nose?
   a. He claimed to be excited and angry about it.
   b. He claimed to be calm and patient about it.
4. What was the insect?
   a. A bee.
   b. A mosquito.
5. What happened when he discovered what it was?
   a. He remained perfectly calm.
   b. He got excited and angry.

C. Write this story, putting one word in each blank space. You will find all the correct words in the story on page 46.

Mr. Williams was famous for his bad temper. When something _____ him, which happened quite often, he used to _____ his arms around in the air and begin to _____ , using the rudest words he knew, which was _____ bad for his children, because they learned to do the same thing.

His wife was very different: she was a quiet, _____ woman who knew the _____ of _____ calm under all circumstances, to avoid wasting one's _____ uselessly. She tried to _____ her children to do this too, and sometimes made them sit down and listen to a _____ about the need for patience.

24 Two businessmen were invited to dinner at the home of a college professor. One of the men did not have much education and was worried that he might make a fool of himself, but his friend said, "Don't worry. Just do what I do, and don't talk about anything that you don't really understand."

The first man managed to get through the dinner successfully, but by the end of the evening he had had a lot to drink, and began to get careless.

A guest asked him whether he liked Shakespeare, and he answered confidently, "It's very pleasant, but I prefer scotch." There was an uncomfortable silence in the room, and soon people began to leave.

When the two friends were out of the house, the second man said to his friend, "You certainly made a fool of yourself making that silly remark about scotch."

"What do you mean?" asked the other man. "What was wrong with it?"

"Everybody knows that Shakespeare isn't a drink," his friend replied. "It's a kind of cheese."

A. Answer these questions:

1. Where were the two businessmen invited?
2. Why was one of them worried?
3. What happened to the businessman by the end of the evening?

Outside the 2,075 words: scotch

4. What did a guest ask him?
5. What did he answer?
6. What did his friend say to him after they had left?
7. What was his friend's opinion on the subject?
8. Who was Shakespeare really?

B. Write these sentences, choosing the correct words under each blank space.

1. The businessmen's reason _____ to the professor's house was
                               (for going)

                               (to go)

_____ him to help them with a new proposal.
(for persuading)
(to persuade)

2. The possibility _____ so had been pointed out to them by a friend,
                      (of his doing)

                      (to do)

whose efforts _____ them together were finally successful.
(of bringing)
(to bring)

3. The professor asked his wife's opinion _____ the businessmen to
                                        (about inviting)

                                        (to invite)

dinner because she had the reputation _____ a good hostess.
(of being)
(to be)

4. Her tendency _____ along with businessmen was good, and
                  (of getting)

                  (to get)

her husband said that her ability _____ so was important.
(of doing)
(to do)

C. Draw lines from the words on the left to the correct words on the right. Then write out the five complete sentences.

1. The professor	a. asked one of the businessmen about Shakespeare.
2. The man whose friend had made a fool of himself	b. gave a dinner party.
3. One of the businessmen	c. was a famous poet and writer.
4. A guest	d. thought that Shakespeare was a kind of cheese.
5. Shakespeare	e. thought that Shakespeare was a drink.

25 Senior citizens are permitted to travel cheaply on a bus if they have a special card. Women may get the card when they are sixty.

Mrs. Matthews lived in the country but she went into town once a week to buy food and other things for the house, and she usually went by bus. She always had to pay the full price for her ride.

Then she reached the age of sixty and got her senior citizen's card, but when she used it for the first time on the bus, it made her feel very old.

The bus driver had often seen her traveling on the bus before, and he noticed that she was feeling unhappy, so after she had paid her money, he winked at her and whispered, "Don't forget to give your mother's card back to her when you see her again."

Mrs. Matthews was very happy when she heard this.

A. Answer these questions:

1. What are senior citizens allowed to do?
2. Where did Mrs. Matthews go once a week?
3. How did she travel?
4. How much did she have to pay for the bus ride before she was sixty?
5. What happened when Mrs. Matthews got her special card?
6. What did the bus driver say to her?
7. Why did he say this?
8. How did Mrs. Matthews feel about this?

Outside the 2,075 words: senior, wink (v.)

B. Which words in the story mean the same as:

1. allowed
2. arrived at
3. at a reduced price
4. closed one eye
5. sad
6. talked softly

C. Write the sentence for each picture, choosing the correct word under each blank space.

1. This woman isn't old enough to travel cheaply on the bus, but she has a card. She _____ have borrowed her mother's card.
   (must)
   (should)

2. She _____ have paid the full amount: it wasn't honest not to.
   (must)
   (should)

3. She _____ be about fifty years old.
   (must)
   (should)

4. She _____ be ashamed of herself.
   (must)
   (should)

5. There seemed to be a lot of other people _____ on the bus that day too.
   (traveled)
   (traveling)

6. The bus hit a brick wall, but no one was _____ .
   (hurt)
   (hurting)

7. Luckily, nobody had been _____ up at the time of the accident.
   (standing)
   (stood)

26 Mr. Thompson did not learn to drive a car until he was almost thirty, because he was a very nervous person who always had the convenience of someone else to drive him—first his mother and then his wife. But at last he decided to take lessons, and managed to pass his driving test on the second attempt, although he still wasn't very good at parking.

A week later he drove into town by himself and was trying to park between two other cars when he damaged one of them slightly.

When he wrote to the insurance company about the accident, they sent him a form to fill in describing it, and one of the questions on the form was, "How could the driver of the other car have prevented the accident from happening?"

Mr. Thompson thought for a minute and then wrote, "He could have parked his car on another street."

A. Answer these questions:

1. Why didn't Mr. Thompson learn to drive sooner?
2. When did he pass his driving test?
3. How did he have an accident?
4. Who did he write to then?
5. What did they do?
6. What was one of the questions Mr. Thompson had to answer?
7. How did he answer the question?

B. Which words in the story mean the opposite of:

1. calm
2. caused
3. fail
4. repaired
5. going forward
6. severely

C. Complete the second sentence in each group, and also the third, where there is one (all the sentences in each group have the same meaning):

Example: a. Mr. Thompson damaged another car.
  b. Another car was damaged by Mr. Thompson.

1. a. The insurance company sent Mr. Thompson a form to fill in.
   b. Mr. Thompson _____.
   c. A form _____.
2. a. Mr. Thompson's mother used to drive him around in her car.
   b. Mr. Thompson _____.
3. a. Two people had parked cars on the street where Mr. Thompson wanted to park.
   b. Cars _____.
4. a. The accident was caused by Mr. Thompson.
   b. Mr. Thompson _____.
5. a. Mr. Thompson had been given a driving test by an official examiner.
   b. An official examiner _____.
   c. A driving test _____.

27 One evening Mrs. Alda asked her husband to take her to a very expensive restaurant in the city, because a lot of movie stars and other famous people ate there, and she was curious to see some of them.

Soon after Mr. and Mrs. Alda had ordered their meal, a very attractive man and woman came into the restaurant and sat down at a table nearby. They were beautifully dressed, and Mrs. Alda said to her husband, "Look at those people, George! I'm sure I've seen their pictures somewhere."

The man and woman gave their order to the waiter, and when he brought Mr. and Mrs. Alda their soup, Mrs. Alda said to him, "Who are those people? Do you know them?"

"Oh, they're nobody famous," he answered at once.

"Really?" Mrs. Alda asked with surprise. "How do you know that?"

"Because they asked me who *you* were," he answered.

A. Answer these questions:

1. Why did Mrs. Alda want to go to the expensive restaurant?
2. Who came into the restaurant after Mr. and Mrs. Alda?
3. What did they look like?
4. What did Mrs. Alda say to her husband?

5. What did she ask the waiter?
6. What did the waiter answer?
7. What did Mrs. Alda say then?
8. What did the waiter tell her?

B. Complete this puzzle:

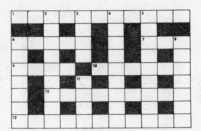

Across:

1. The people who came into the restaurant after Mr. and Mrs. Alda were _____ dressed.
6. Mrs. Alda thought that the man might be a famous _____.
7. Before dinner Mr. and Mrs. Alda had a drink at the _____.
9. The young performer _____ into a famous actor.
10. People who compete with each other.
12. Forcing someone to stop speaking.
13. Places where people go to have dinner.

Down:

2. Mrs. Alda wanted to see some famous actors and _____ .
3. Mr. Alda took a taxi because his car had a flat _____ .
4. That person is not from this country. He must be a _____.
5. The school _____ helped me find the books I needed.
6. Being more mad or annoyed.
8. When a person does not want to do a particular job anymore, he _____ .
11. The last name of the people in this story.

C. Write this story, using words instead of the pictures:

Before Mrs. Alda went out, she her hair,

her and powdered her She did not have

much , but she put on her ring, her gold

, and her pearl Then she put on her

 , which had a small on it, and went out

to meet her husband at the restaurant.

28 An artist who did not have much money, but was a very kind man, was coming home by train one day. He gave his last few coins to a beggar, but then he saw another one, and forgot that he did not have any money. He asked the man if he would like to have lunch with him, and the beggar accepted, so they went into a small restaurant and had a good meal.

At the end, the artist could not pay the bill, of course, so the beggar had to do so.

The artist was very unhappy about this, so he said to the beggar, "Come home with me in a taxi, my friend, and I'll give you back the money for lunch."

"Oh, no!" the beggar answered quickly. "I had to pay for your lunch, but I'm not going to pay for your taxi home too!"

A. Answer these questions:

1. What kind of man was the artist?
2. What had he forgotten about?
3. What did he ask the beggar to do?
4. Where did they go after that?
5. What happened at the end of the meal?

6. What did the artist say then?
7. What did the beggar answer?

B. Which of these sentences are true? Write down the correct ones.

1. The artist in this story invited a beggar to have lunch with him.
2. The artist in this story asked a beggar to give him lunch.
3. The beggar thought that he would have to pay the bill.
4. The beggar didn't expect to pay the bill.
5. The artist wanted the beggar to come home with him by taxi so they could have lunch together.
6. The artist wanted the beggar to come home with him by taxi so he could pay him back for the lunch.
7. The artist was going to pay for the taxi ride when he got home.
8. The artist didn't want to pay for the taxi ride himself.
9. The beggar thought that the artist wanted to have a free taxi ride.
10. The beggar thought that the artist would pay for the taxi when he got home.

C. Write the number of the correct sentence under each picture:

1. He gave a beggar his last few coins.
2. He took him to a restaurant.
3. The beggar paid the bill for lunch.
4. The beggar refused to get in, because he didn't want to pay for that too.
5. Then he met another beggar on the street.
6. Then the artist took the beggar to a taxi.
7. An artist got out of a train one day.
8. When the waiter brought the bill, the artist could not pay it.

29 The students at a certain American university used to play tricks on each other when one of them was going to receive his first visit from a new girlfriend. Usually the trick was to take all the furniture out of the student's room, so that when his girlfriend arrived, there was nothing to sit on.

Ted Jones was a country boy who had never left his birthplace until his admission to the university. When he arrived there for the first time and heard about this behavior, he disliked it and announced to the other students, "I'm determined that that's not going to happen to me. I'm going to lock my door." His confident words were greeted with laughter by the other students.

When Ted brought his girlfriend to his room for the first time, he was astonished to find that all the furniture was there—but the door of his room was gone.

A. Answer these questions:

1. When did the students play tricks on each other?
2. What was the usual trick?
3. What kind of person was Ted Jones?
4. What did he think of the students' tricks?
5. What did he say very confidently?
6. How did the other students answer?
7. What happened when Ted brought his girlfriend to his room?

B. Which of these answers are correct? Write down the questions and the correct answers.

1. Did the students in this story know in advance when a new girlfriend was going to visit one of their friends?
   a. Yes, they did.
   b. No, they didn't.
2. What did they usually do then?
   a. They changed all the student's furniture around.
   b. They removed the student's furniture from the room.
3. What would the girlfriend then find when she arrived?
   a. She would find that the chairs were too uncomfortable to sit on.
   b. She would find that there were no chairs.
4. What did Ted Jones decide to do when he heard about this?
   a. He decided to lock his door.
   b. He decided to take his door away.
5. What did his girlfriend find when she arrived?
   a. That all the furniture had been taken away.
   b. That the door of Ted's room was missing.

C. Write this story, putting one word in each blank space. You will find all the correct words in the story on page 58.

Mary was born in 1962. Her _____ was a small town in California. She was a bright girl, and her _____ to a good university at the age of seventeen was no surprise to her parents, who had always been _____ of her ability.

Mary was a serious student, and was _____ to do well in her studies. She strongly _____ the kind of silly _____ many of her classmates thought funny, and never joined in their _____ at these jokes.

Her professors _____ that she was the best student they had ever had, and when she went up to _____ her degree, after passing her exams with extraordinarily high marks, their applause was nearly deafening.

They were, therefore, quite _____ to find that she later gave up her studies to sail around the world in a small boat!

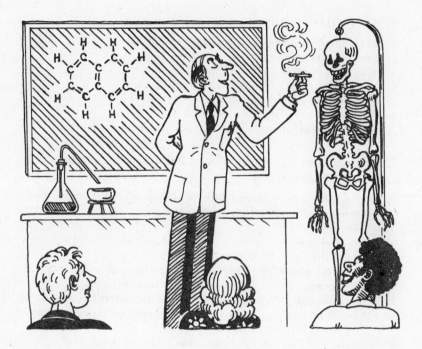

30 George and Carol were medical students at the same college and, like many other college students, they enjoyed playing jokes on people. Both of them smoked, but they knew that their professors were strongly against it, because smoking was dangerous to one's health. One day they decided to play a joke on their professor.

At one of their medical lectures there was always a skeleton in the room so that the professor could show the students the different bones in the human body.

That afternoon, Carol and George put a cigarette in the mouth of the skeleton that was to be used for their next lecture.

When the professor came in, he began talking and then noticed the cigarette. He went up to the skeleton, took the cigarette out of its mouth and said, "You really should give them up, old boy. Look what they're doing to you!"

Outside the 2,075 words: skeleton

A. Answer these questions:

1. What were George and Carol studying?
2. What did they both enjoy?
3. What did their professors think about smoking?
4. What was in one of the lecture rooms?
5. Why was it there?
6. What did Carol and George do one afternoon?
7. What did the professor do when he noticed this?
8. And what did he say?

B. Write these sentences, putting *about, at, for, in, of, on, out of, to, with, within,* **or** *without* **in each blank space.**

1. The students are working hard _____ preparation _____ their medical examinations.
2. They can ask their teachers questions about anything they are _____ doubt _____ .
3. However, they must keep _____ the limits _____ the exam subjects.
4. Also, if something is _____ interest _____ any but a few students, the teacher often refers them to a book for the answer.
5. The university was closed yesterday _____ respect _____ the oldest professor, who had just died.
6. It may be difficult for all the students to get here by 9:00 a.m. _____ account _____ the heavy traffic in town.
7. Some of them may come before the rush hour, _____ the risk _____ being tired before the exam begins.
8. Some students who cannot leave until later will be _____ danger _____ being late.
9. _____ the surprise _____ all of us, no students were late last year.
10. _____ regard _____ our plans for next year, we want to try a later time for starting each day's exams.

C. Draw lines from the words on the left to the correct words on the right. Then write out the five complete sentences.

1. George and Carol

2. One of the medical lectures

3. Smoking

4. The professor

5. The skeleton

a. advised the skeleton to stop smoking.

b. put a cigarette in the skeleton's mouth.

c. was used for medical lectures.

d. was disapproved of by the professors.

e. was about bones.

61

2075 Word Vocabulary

Note: This vocabulary does not contain numerals, names of the days of the week, names of the months or proper nouns and adjectives. Not all cases of nouns and pronouns are given (e.g. *boy* stands for *boy—boy's—boys—boys'*); nor are all parts of verbs given (e.g. *swim* stands for *swim—swims—swam—swum—swimming*). Comparatives and superlatives of adjectives are not given.

a(n)
(un)able (ability, enable)
about
above
abroad
absent (absence)
absolute
accept(ed)
accident(al)
according
account
accurate
accuse (accusation)
accustom
ache
acid
across
act(ing, ion, ive,
   ivity, or, ress)
actual
add(ition)
address
admire (admiration)
admit (admission)
adopt(ed)
adult
advance(d)
(dis)advantage
adventure
advertise(ment)
advice (advise)
affair
affect
afford
afraid
after
afternoon
again
against
age
agent (agency)
ago
(dis)agree(ment)
agriculture
ahead
aim(less)
air(-force, -line, -mail,
   -plane, -port)

algebra
all
allow(ance)
almost
alone
along(-side)
already
also
although
altogether
always
a.m.
ambition (ambitious)
ambulance
among
amount
amuse(ment) (amusing)
anchor
ancient
and
anger (angry)
angle
animal
ankle
announce(d)
annoy(ance)
answer
ant
anxious (anxiety)
any(-more)
apart
apartment
apology (apologize)
(dis)appear(ance)
applaud (applause)
apple
apply (application)
appoint(ment)
(dis)approve (approval)
arch(ed, -way)
argue (argument)
arm
army
around
arrange(ment)
arrest
arrive (arrival)
arrow

art(ist(ic), -school)
article
artificial
as
ash(-tray)
ashamed
ask
asleep
association
astonish(ed, ing, ment)
at
attack
attempt
attend(ance, ant)
   (attention, attentive)
attract(ion, ive)
audience
aunt
autumn
avenue
average
avoid(ance)
   (unavoidable)
awake(n)
away
awkward(ness)
axe

baby
back (*a.*)
back(-bone, -ground,
   wards)
bad (worse/worst)
bag
baggage
bake(r)
balance
ball
balloon
banana
band(-stand)
bandage
bank(er)
bar
barber
bare(-headed)
bargain
bark

barrel
base
basis
basket
bath(-room, -tub)
bathe
bathing (-suit)
battery
battle
bay
be(ing)
beach
bead
beak
beam
bean
bear
beard
beast
beat(en, ing)
beautiful (beauty)
because
become
bed(-room)
bee
beer
before
beg(gar)
begin(ning)
behave (behavior)
behind
believe (belief)
bell
belong
below
belt
bench
bend
beneath
berry
beside(s)
between
beyond
bicycle
big
bill
bind(ing)
bird

birth(-day, -place)
bit
bite
bitter(ness)
black
blackboard
blade
blame
blanket
bless(ed, ing)
blind(ing)
block
blood (bleed)
blouse
blow
blue
blunt
board
boast(ful)
boat
body(-guard) (bodily,
  also -body, e.g. in
  anybody)
boil(er)
bold(ness)
bomb
bone
book(-case)
boot
border
born
borrow
both
bottle
bottom
boundary
bounds (unbounded)
bow(-tie)
bow (v.)
bowl
box
boy (-friend)
bracelet
brain
brake
branch
brass
brave(ry)
bread
break
breakfast
breath(e)
bribe(ry)
brick
bridge
bright(en)
bring
broad(en)
broadcast
broken
brother
brown
bruise
brush

bucket
build(ing)
bullet
bulletin
bunch
bundle
burn(ing)
burst
bury (burial)
bus (-stop)
bush(y)
business (-man, -like)
busy
but
butter(-dish)
butterfly
button(-hole)
buy(er)
by

cabbage
cabinet
cage
cake
(mis)calculate (calculation)
call
calm
camera
camp
can
canal
candle
candy
cap
cape
capital
captain
car
card
cardboard
care
careful
careless
carpet
carriage
carry
cart
case
castle
cat
catch(ing)
cause
caution (cautious)
cave
ceiling
celebrate(d)
  (celebration)
cent
center (central)
century
ceremony
(un)certain(ly, ty)
chain
chair(-man, -woman)

chalk
chance
change
character
charcoal
charge
charm(ing)
cheap
cheat
check(-book)
cheek
cheer(ful, ing)
cheese
chemical (chemistry)
chest
chew
chicken
chief
child(ish, -hood, -like)
chimney
chin
chocolate
choose (choice)
Christmas
church
cigarette
circle (circular)
circus
citizen
city
civilized
  (civilization)
claim
class(-room)
classify
  (classification)
clay
clean(liness)
clear(ness)
clerk
clever
cliff
climate
climb(er, ing)
clock(-work)
close (a.)
close(d)
closet
cloth
clothes (clothing)
cloud(y)
club
coal(-mine)
coarse
coast(-line)
coat (-rack)
cock
coffee(-pot)
coin
cold(ness)
collar
collect(tion, or)
college
colony (colonial)

color(ed, ing)
column
comb
combine(d)
  (combination)
come
(un)comfortable
  (comforting,
  discomfort)
command(er)
commerce (commercial)
committee
(un)common
company (companion)
compare (comparison)
compete (competition,
  competitor)
complain(t)
complete
complicated
compose(r)
  (composition)
concern(ing)
condition
confess(ion)
confident (confidence)
confidential
confuse(d)
  (confusion)
congratulate
connect(ion)
conquer(ed, ing)
conscience
(un)conscious(ness)
consider(ation, ing)
contain(er)
(dis)content(ed)
continue (continual,
  continuous)
control
(in)convenient
conversation(al)
cook(ed, ing)
cookie
cool(ness)
copper
copy
cork(-screw)
corn
corner
correct(ion)
  (incorrect)
cost
cottage
cotton
cough
council
count
country
courage(ous)
course
court(-yard)
cousin
cover(ed, ing)

63

cow
coward(ice, ly)
crack(ed)
crash
crawl
cream
creature
creep
crime (criminal)
critic(al, ism, ize)
crop
cross(ing)
crowd(ed)
cruel(ty)
crush(ing)
cry
cultivate(d)
  (cultivation)
cup
cure
curious (curiosity)
curl(ed, y)
current
curse
curtain
curve(d)
cushion(ed)
custom
cut(ting)

daddy
damage(d)
damp
dance(-band)
danger(ous)
dare(daring)
dark(en, ness)
date
daughter
day(-light, -time)
  (daily)
dead (death)
deaf(en(ing))
deal
dean
dear
debt
decay
deceive (deceit(ful))
decide (decision)
deck
declare (declaration)
decorate (decoration)
decrease
deed
deep(en) (depth)
deer
defeat
defend(ant) (defense)
degree
delay
delicate
delight(ed, ful)
deliver(y)

demand
dentist
department
depend(ant)
  (dependence)
descend(ant)
  (descent)
describe (description)
desert
deserve (deserving)
desire
desk
despair (desperate)
destroy (destruction,
  destructive)
detail(ed)
determine(d)
  (determination)
develop(ment)
diamond
dictionary
die
differ(ent, ence)
difficult(y)
dig
dining(-hall, -room)
dinner
dip
direct(ion, or)
dirt(y)
disappoint(ed, ing,
  ment)
discipline
discover(er, y)
discuss(ion)
disease(d)
disgust(ed, ing)
dish
dismiss(al)
distant (distance)
distinguish(ed, ing)
district
disturb(ance, ed)
ditch
dive(r)
divide (division)
do
doctor
dog
dollar
donkey
door(-way)
dorm(itory)
dot
double
doubt(ful, less)
down(-hill)
dozen
drag
draw(ing)
drawer
dream(y)
dress
drill

drink
drive(r)
drop
drown
drug(gist, -store)
drum(mer)
drunk
dry(ness)
duck
due
dull
dumb
during
dust(y)
duster
duty

each
eager(ness)
ear(-ring)
early
earnest
earn(ings)
earth(-quake)
ease
east(ern)
Easter
easy
eat
edge
educate (education(al))
effect(ive)
efficient (efficiency)
effort
egg
either
elastic(ity)
elect(ion)
electric(al, ian, ity)
elephant
else
employ(ee, er, ment)
  (unemployed)
empty
enclose (enclosure)
encourage(ment)
end(ing, less)
enemy
engine (engineer)
enjoy(able, ment)
enough
enter (entrance)
entertain(ing, ment)
entire
entrust
envelope
envy (envious)
equal(ity)
escape
essence (essential)
even
evening
event

ever (and -ever, e.g. in
  whoever)
every(-day, -where)
evil
exact
examine (examination,
  examiner)
example
excellent (excellence)
except(ion)
excess(ive)
exchange
excite(d, ment)
  (exciting)
excuse
exercise
exist(ence, ing)
expect(ation)
expense (expensive)
experience(d)
  (inexperienced)
experiment(al)
explain (explanation)
explode (explosion)
explore(r) (exploration)
express(ion)
extend (extent,
  extension)
extra
extraordinary
extreme
eye(-brow, -lash, -lid,
  -sight)

face(-powder)
fact
factory
fade
fail(ure)
faint(ness)
(un)fair(ness)
faith(ful(ly))
fall(ing)
false
fame(famous)
familiar
family
fan
fancy (fanciful)
far(-reaching)
farm(er)
farther (farthest)
fashion(able)
fast
fasten(er)
fat(ness, ten)
fate (fatal)
father
faucet
fault(less, y)
favor(able, ite)
fear(ful, less)
feast(ing)
feather

64

feed
feel(ing)
fellow(ship)
female
fence
fever(ish)
few
field
fierce
fight(er)
figure
fill
film
final(ly)
find
fine(ness)
finger
finish(ed)
fire(-man, -place)
firm(ness)
first
fish(erman)
fit(ness, ting)
fix
flag
flame (flaming)
flash(ing)
flat(ten)
flavor
flesh
float
flood(ed)
floor
flour
flow
flower
fly (flight)
fog(gy)
(un)fold
follow(er, ing)
fond(ness)
food
fool(ish)
foot(-ball, -path, -print,
   -step)
for
forbid(den)
force(d)
foreign(er)
forest
forget(ful)
forgive(ness)
fork
form
(in)formal(ity)
former
forth
(mis)fortune
   ((un)fortunate)
forward(s)
frame(-work)
free(dom)
freeze (frozen)
frequent

fresh(en, ness)
friend(ly, -ship)
frighten(ed)
from
front
fruit
fry
full
funeral
fun(ny)
fur
furnish(ed)
furniture
further (furthest)
future

gain
gallon
game
gap
garage
garbage
garden(er)
gas
gate(-way)
gather
gay
general
generous (generosity)
gentle(ness)
gentleman
geography
geometry
get
girl(-friend)
give (gift)
glad
glass(es, y)
glory
glue
go
goal
goat
gold(en, -mine)
good(better/best)
goodbye
goodness
govern(ment, or)
grace(ful)
gradual
grain
grammar (grammatical)
grand-
   (e.g. in grandfather)
grape
grass(y)
grateful
grave(-stone)
gray
grease (greasy)
great(ness)
greed(y)
green
greet(ing)

grill
grind
ground
group
grow(n-up)
growl
growth
guard
guess
guest
guide(-book)
   (misguided)
guilt(less, y)
gun

habit
hair(y)
half (halve)
hall
hammer
hand(ful, -bag,
   -shake, -writing)
handkerchief
handle
handsome
hang
happen(ing)
(un)happy (happiness)
harbor
hard(en, ness)
hardly
harm(ful, less)
harvest
hat(-rack)
hate(hatred)
have
hay
he
head(ing)
heal
health(y)
heap
hear(ing)
heart
heaven(ly)
heavy
heel
hello
help(er, ful, ing, less)
hen
here
hesitate (hesitation)
hi
hide
high(-way)
   (height(en))
hill(y, -side)
hinder
hire
history (historic(al))
hit
hobby
hold(er)
hole

holiday
hollow
holy (holiness)
home(less, -made,
   -work)
(dis)honest(y)
honey
(dis)honor(able)
hook
hooray/hurrah
hope(ful, less)
horizon(tal)
horn
horse(-back, -man,
   -shoe)
hospital
host(ess)
hot (heat, heating)
hotel
hour(ly, -hand)
house (-hold,
   -keeper, -wife,
   -work)
how(-ever)
huge
human(ity)
humble
hunger (hungry)
hunt(er, ing)
hurry
hurt
husband
hut

I
ice(-cream) (icy)
idea
ideal
idle(ness)
if
ill(ness)
imagine (imagination,
   imaginative,
   imaginary)
imitate (imitation)
immediate(ly)
important (importance)
improve(d, ment)
in(-to)
inch
include (including,
   inclusive)
increase
indeed
indoor(s)
industry (industrial)
influence (influential)
(in)flu(enza)
inform(ation)
inject(ion)
ink(y)
-in-law (e.g. son-in-
   law)
inner(most)

65

inquire
insect
insensible
inside
instant
instead
instrument
insult(ing)
insure (insurance)
intelligent (intelligence)
intend (intention(al))
interest(ed, ing)
interfere(nce)
interrupt(ion)
introduce
  (introduction)
invent(ion, or)
invite (invitation)
iron
island
it

jam
jar
jaw
jealous(y)
jewel(ry)
job
join(t)
joke
journalist
journey
joy(ful)
judge (judgment)
juice (juicy)
jump
just (*adv.*)
(un)just
(in)justice

keep(er)
key
kick
kill
(un)kind(ness)
king
kiss
kitchen
kite
knee(l)
knife
knit
knock
knot
know(ledge)
(un)known

lack(ing)
ladder
lady
lake
lamp(-shade)
land(ing, -lord)
language

large
last(ing)
late(ness)
lately
laugh(ter)
law(yer)
  ((un)lawful)
lay
lazy (laziness)
lead (led)
lead(er(ship))
  (mislead)
leaf(y)
leak
lean
learn(ed, ing)
least
leather
leave
lecture(r)
left(-hand(ed))
leg
lend (loan)
less(en)
lesson
let
letter
level
liar
liberty
library (librarian)
lick
lid
lie
life(-boat, less, -like,
  -long, -size)
lift
light(en, ness,
  -hearted)
light(er, -house)
(dis)like (alike)
(un)likely
limit(ed)
line
lion
lip(-stick)
liquid
list
listen(er)
literature (literary)
little
(a)live
living-room
(un)load
loaf
local
(un)lock(ed)
log
lonely (loneliness)
long (length)
look
loose(n)
lose (loss, lost)
lot

(a)loud
love(r) (lovable,
  loving)
low(er)
loyal(ty)
luck(y) (unlucky)
luggage
lump
lunch
lung

ma'am
machine(ry)
mad(ness)
magazine
mail
main(-land)
make(r)
male
man(-kind)
manage(r, ment)
manner(s)
manufacture(r)
many
map
marble
march
mark
market
marry (marriage,
  married)
mass
master(y, -piece)
mat
match(-box)
match(ing)
material
math(ematics)
matter
may
maybe
mayor
meal
mean(ing)
mean (-time, -while)
means
measure(ment)
meat
mechanical (mechanism)
medical (medicine)
meet(ing)
melt
member(-ship)
memory (memorial)
mention
menu
merchant
mercy
  (merci(ful, less))
mere(ly)
merry
message (messenger)
metal
middle(-aged)

midnight
mild(ness)
mile(age)
milk(y, -bottle)
mill(er)
mind
mine(r)
mineral
minister (ministry)
minute(-hand)
mirror
misery (miserable)
miss(ing)
Miss
mistake
mix(ed, ture)
model
moderate (moderation)
modern(ize)
modest(y)
moment(ary)
mom(my)
money
monkey
month(ly)
moon(-light)
(im)moral(ity)
more(-over)
morning
mosquito
most(ly)
mother(ly, -hood)
motor(-boat, -cycle)
mountain(ous)
mouse(-trap)
mouth(ful)
move(ment)
  (motion(less))
movie (-star)
Mr(s).
much
mud(dy)
multiply (multiplication)
murder(er)
music(al, ian)
must
mustache
mystery (mysterious)

nail
name(less)
narrow(ness)
nation
  ((inter)national)
native
nature
  ((un)natural)
navy (naval)
near
nearly
neat(ness)
(un)necessary (necessity)
neck
necklace

need
needle
neglect
neighbor(ing, -hood)
neither
nephew
nervous(ness)
nest
net(-work)
never
new
news(-paper)
next
nice
niece
night(ly, -time)
no
noble
nod
noise (noisy)
none
noon
nor
normal
north(ern)
nose
not
note(-book, -paper)
notice(able)
noun
now
nowadays
nuisance
number (numerous)
nurse(ry)
nut

oar
obey (obedient,
    obedience)
object (n.)
object(ion)
observe(r)
    (observation)
occasion(al)
ocean
o'clock
of
off
offend(ed) (offense)
offer
office
officer
official
often
oh
oil(y)
okay
old(-fashioned)
olive
omit (omission)
on(-to)
once

one(-sided)
    (also -one, e.g.
    in anyone)
onion
only
open(ing)
operate (operation)
opinion
opportunity
opposite
or
orange
order(ly)
ordinary
organ
organize(d)
    (organization)
origin(al)
ornament(al)
other(-wise)
ought
ounce
out(-door(s),
    -let, -line, -look,
    -number, -spoken,
    -standing, -weigh)
outer(most)
outside
oven
over(-board,
    -charge, -come,
    -flow, -grown,
    -joyed, -look)
overcoat
owe
own(er (-ship))

pack(age, ed, ing)
packet
pad(ded, ding)
page
pain(ful)
paint(er, ing)
pair
pale(ness)
pan
pants
paper
pardon
parent
park
part(ing, ly, -time)
particular
partner
party
pass(ing)
passage(-way)
passenger
passport
past
paste
pastry
path
(im)patient (patience)

patriotic
pattern
pause
paw
pay(ment) (unpaid)
peace(ful)
pearl
peculiar
pen
pencil(-box)
penny
people
per
perfect(ion)
perform(ance, er)
perhaps
permanent
permit (permission)
person(al)
persuade (persuasion)
pet
phonograph
photograph(er, ic, y)
physics
piano
pick
picnic
picture
piece
pig
pile
pillow
pilot
pin
pinch
pink
pint
pipe
pity
place
plain
plan
plant(er)
plaster
plate
play(er, -ground)
(un)pleasant
please(d) (pleasure)
plenty (plentiful)
plow
plural
p.m.
pocket(-book)
poem (poet(ic, ry))
point(ed, er)
poison(ous)
police(-man)
polish
polite(ness)
politics (political,
    politician)
pond
pool
poor (poverty)

popular(ity)
population
port
porter
position
possess(ion)
(im)possible (possibility)
post(age (stamp),
    -card, -man,
    -office)
postpone
pot
potato
pound
pour
powder(y, -puff)
power(ful)
practical
practice
praise
pray
preach(er)
precious
prefer(able, ence)
prejudice
prepare (preparation)
present (n. & v.)
present (presence)
preserve
president
press
pressure
pretend (pretense)
pretty
prevent(ion)
price
priest
prince(ss)
print(ed, er)
prison(er)
private
prize(d)
probable (probability)
problem
procession
produce(r) (product
    (ion, ive))
profession(al)
professor
profit
program
progress
promise (promising)
prompt(ness)
pronounce
    (pronunciation)
proof
(im)proper
property
propose (proposal)
protect(ion)
proud (pride)
prove
provide

public
pull
pump
punctual
punish(ment)
pupil
im)pure
purple
purpose
purse
push(ing)
put
puzzle (puzzling)

qualify (qualified,
   qualification)
quality
quantity
quarrel(-some)
quart
quarter(ly)
queen
question(-mark)
quick(ness)
quiet(ness)
quite

rabbit
race(-track, -horse)
racket
radio
rail(ing, -road)
rain(y, -bow, -coat,
   -fall, -water)
raise
rank
rapid
rare
rash
rat
rate
rather
raw(ness)
ray
razor
reach
read(er)
ready(-made)
real(ity)
realize (realization)
reason(able)
receive(r) (receipt)
recent
recite
recognize (recognition)
recommend(ation)
record player
red(den, dish, -hot)
reduce (reduction)
refer(ence)
reflect(ion)

refresh(ing, ment(s))
refrigerator
refuse (refusal)
(dis)regard (regarding,
   regardless)
regret
(ir)regular(ity)
rejoice
relation
relative
relieve (relief)
religion (religious)
remain(ing)
remark
remedy
remember
remind
rent
repair
repeat(ed)
replace
reply
report(er)
represent(ative)
republic
reputation
request
rescue
reserve
resign(ation)
resist(ance)
(dis)respect(ful)
   (respectable)
responsible
   (responsibility)
rest(less)
restaurant
result(ing)
retire(ment)
return
revenge
review
reward
ribbon
rice
rich(es)
rid
ride(r)
rifle
right(-angle,
   -hand(ed))
ring
ripe(n)
rise (rising, arise)
risk(y)
rival(ry)
river(-side)
road(-side)
roar
roast
rob(ber(y))
rock(y)

rod
roll(er, ing)
roof
room
root(ed)
rope
rose
rotten
rough(ness)
round
row
rub
rubber
rude(ness)
rug
ruin(ed)
rule (ruling)
ruler
run(ner, ning)
rush(ing)
rust(y)

sack
sacred
sacrifice
sad(den, ness)
saddle
safe(ty)
sail(ing-ship)
sailor
sake
salary
salesman
salt(y)
same
sample
sand(y, -bank,
   -dune)
sandwich
(dis)satisfy
   (satisfaction)
   ((un)satisfactory)
sauce
saucer
sausage
save(saving)
saw(-dust, -mill)
say(ing)
scale(s)
scarce
scatter
scene(ry)
scent(ed)
school
science (scientist,
   scientific)
scissors
scold(ing)
score
scorn(ful)
scout
scrape

scratch
screen
screw(-driver)
   (unscrew)
sea(-coast, -level,
   -man, -port,
   -shell, -shore,
   -water, -weed)
search(ing)
season
seat
second (n.)
second (-hand)
secret (secrecy)
secretary
see
seed
seem
seize
seldom
self(-conscious(ness),
   -contained, -control,
   -defense, -governing,
   -respect)
self, -selves,
   (e.g. in myself,
   ourselves)
(un)selfish
sell(er)
send
sense (sensible,
   sensation,
   (in)sensitive,
   nonsense)
sentence
separate (separation)
serious(ness)
servant
serve (service)
set
settle(r, ment)
several
severe
sew(ing)
shade (shady)
shadow(y)
shake
shall
shallow(ness)
shame(ful, less)
shape(less)
share
sharp(en, ness)
shave (shaving-
   brush, soap)
she
shed
sheep
sheet
shelf
shell(-fish)
shelter

shield
shine
ship(ment, -wreck)
shirt
shock(ed, ing)
shoe(-maker)
shoot (shot)
shop
(a)shore
short(en, ness)
shorts
shoulder
shout
show
shower
shut
shy(ness)
sick(ness)
side(-ways) (aside)
sight(-seeing)
sign
signal
signature
silent (silence)
silk(y, -worm)
silly
silver(y)
simple (simplicity)
since
sincere
sing(er)
single (singular)
sink
sir
sister
sit
situation
size
skill(ed, ful)
skin
skirt
sky
slave(ry)
sleep(y, er, iness, less)
slice
slide (sliding)
slight
slip(pery)
slope (sloping)
slow(ness)
smack
small(ness)
smart
smell
smile
smoke (smoky,
   smoking-section)
smooth(ness)
snake
snow(y, -ball, -storm)
so
soap(y)

social (society)
sock
soft(en, ness)
soil
soldier
solemn
solid
solve (solution)
some(-how)
sometimes
son
song(-book)
soon
sore
sorrow(ful)
sorry
sort
soul
sound
soup
sour
south(ern)
sow
space
spade
spare
speak(er) (speech)
special
speed
spell(ing)
spend
spill
spin
spirit
spit
spite
splash
splendid
split
spoil(ed)
spoon(ful)
sport(sman)
spot(less)
spread
spring(-time)
square
squat
staff
stage
stain
stairs (staircase)
   (also -stairs, e.g.
   in upstairs)
stale
stamp (-album,
   -collector)
stand
standard(ize)
star
start
state(ment)
station

stay
(un)steady
steal
steam(er, -boat,
   -engine, -ship)
steel
steep
steer(ing-wheel)
stem
step
stick
sticky
stiff(en, ness)
still(ness)
sting
stir(ring)
stock
stocking
stomach
stone
stop (non-stop)
store(-house, -room)
storm(y)
story
stove
straight(en)
strange(r, ness)
strap
straw
stream
street
stretch
strict
strike
string
strip
stripe(d)
stroke
strong (strength(en))
struggle
student
study
stuff
stupid(ity)
subject
submarine
substance
succeed (success(ful))
such
suck
sudden(ly)
suffer(er, ing)
sugar(-bowl)
suggest(ion)
suit(able)
suit(-case)
sum
summer(-time)
sun(ny, -burn, -light,
   -rise, -set, -shine)
supper
supply

support
suppose
sure
surface
surprise(d)
   (surprising)
surround(ing)
suspect (suspicion,
   suspicious)
swallow
swear
sweat
sweep
sweet(en, ness)
swell(ing) (swollen)
swim(mer, ming-pool)
swing(ing)
switch
sword
sympathy (sympathize,
   sympathetic)
system

table(-spoon)
tail
tailor
take
talk
tall
tame
tank
tap
taste(less)
tax
taxi
tea(-cup, -pot, -spoon)
teach(er)
team
tear
telegram (telegraph)
telephone
telescope
television (T.V.)
tell(er)
temper
temperature
temple
tempt(ation)
tend(ency)
tender(ness)
tennis
tent
term
terrible
test
than
thank(ful) (thanks)
that/those
that (conj.)
the
theater (theatrical)

then
there
therefore
thermometer
they
thick(en, ness)
thief
thin(ness)
thing (also -thing, e.g. in nothing)
think(er)
thirst(y)
this/these
thorn(y)
thorough
thought(ful(ness))
thread
threat(en(ing))
throat
through
throw
thumb
thunder
thus
ticket
tide (tidal)
tidy
tie (untie)
tiger
tight(en)
till
time(-table)
tin
tip
tire
tired (tiring)
title
to
tobacco
today
toe
together
tomorrow
ton
tongue
tonight
too
tool
tooth(-paste)
top
torch
total
touch
tough
tour(ist)
toward(s)
towel
tower
town
toy
track
trade(-mark)
traffic

train (n.)
train(ed, ing)
translate (translator, translation)
transparent
trap(ped, ping)
travel(er)
tray
treasure(r) (treasury)
treat(ment)
tree
tremble
tribe
trick
trip
trouble(-some)
truck
true (truth(ful))
trumpet
trunk
trust(ed) (distrust)
try (trial)
tube
tune
tunnel
turn(ing)
twice
twin
twist
type(-writer)
typist

ugly (ugliness)
umbrella
uncle
under(neath, -ground, -line)
(mis)understand(ing)
union
unit
unite (unity)
universe (universal)
university
unless
until
up(-hill, on, set, -side-down)
urge(nt)
use(ful, less)
used to
usually

vacation
vain
valley
value (valuable)
van
vary (various, variety)
vase
vegetable
veil
verb

verse
vertical
very
vessel
vest
victory
view
village
violent (violence)
violin
virtue
visit(or)
voice
volcano
volley-ball
vote(r)
voyage

wage(s)
waist
wait(ing-room)
waiter (waitress)
wake
walk
wall
wallet
wander
want
war(-ship)
-ward(s) (e.g. in backward(s))
warm(th)
warn(ing)
wash(ing)
waste(ful)
watch(-dog, -man)
water(y, -fall, -pipe, -proof)
wave (wavy)
wax
way
we
weak(en, ness)
wealth(y)
weapon
wear (worn-out)
weather
weave
wedding
weed
week(ly, -day, -end)
weigh(t)
welcome
well(-being)
west(ern)
wet
what
wheat
wheel
when(-ever)
where (also -where, e.g. in somewhere)

whether
which
while
whip
whisper
whistle
white(n, ness, -wash)
who
whole
why
wicked(ness)
wide(n, -awake, -spread) (width)
widow(er)
wife
wild
will (n.)
(un)willing(ness)
win
wind(y)
window
wine
wing
winter (-time)
wipe
wire
wise (wisdom)
wish
with(-out)
within
witness
woman
wonder(ful)
wood(ed, en, -land, -work)
wool(len)
word
work(er, ing(s), -shop)
world(-famous, -wide)
worm
worry (worried, worrying)
worship
worth(less)
wound(ed)
wrap(ped, per)
wreck
wrist(-watch)
write(r, ing) (written)
wrong(-doing)

yard
year(ly)
yellow
yes
yesterday
yet
yield(ing)
you
young (youth(ful))

zero
zoo

Grammatical Structures

The grammatical structures used in this book are limited to the following:

1. **Present continuous:** *am/are/is + verb + ing* to indicate an action or state going on at the time that it is being spoken or written about. *Example:* I am reading a story.
2. **Present continuous:** *am/are/is doing* for a relatively temporary present habit. *Example:* She is watching T.V.
3. **Present continuous:** *am/are/is (always) doing* for habitual and irritating action. *Example:* He is always playing the stereo when I want to study.
4. **Simple present:** to indicate an action or state going on at the time it is being spoken or written about; used with certain involuntary verbs. *Example:* I feel well.
5. **Simple present:** to express habitual action. *Example:* I get up at seven every morning.
6. **Present perfect:** *have/has done* to indicate an action or state completed at some unspecified past time. *Example:* I have finished my homework.
7. **Present perfect:** *have/has done* to indicate an action or state which began some time in the past and has continued to the moment of speaking. *Example:* He has worked here for six months.
8. **Present perfect continuous:** *have/has been doing* to indicate an action which began in the past and is still continuing. *Example:* He has been playing the piano for eight years.
9. **Simple past:** to indicate a past action or state, when the speaker or writer is referring to the time of the completed action or state. *Example:* I finished my work at five-thirty.
10. **Past continuous:** *was/were doing* to indicate an action or state begun before, and continuing after, a particular moment in the past. *Example:* I was having my lunch (when you called).
11. **Past continuous:** *was/were doing* to indicate parallel actions or states in the past. *Example:* While I was reading, John was writing.

12. **Past continuous:** *was/were doing* for a relatively temporary past habit. *Example:* She was watching T.V. last night.
13. **Past continuous:** *was/were doing* for habitual and irritating action in the past. *Example:* He was always playing the stereo when I wanted to study.
14. **Habitual past:** *used to + verb* to indicate habitual past action no longer going on at the present time. *Example:* When I was younger, I used to play the piano.
15. **Past perfect:** *had done* to indicate an action completed before or at a specified time in the past. *Example:* He had lived there for six years before moving to the city.
16. **Past perfect continuous:** *had been doing* for continuous action up to a specified past time. *Example:* She had been waiting for the bus for half an hour.
17. **Future be + going to:** *am/are/is going to do* to indicate future actions or states. *Example:* I'm going to drive to New York next Monday.
18. **Future with will:** to indicate future actions. *Example:* (Don't do that, or) you'll hurt yourself.
19. **Present continuous:** *am/are/is + verb + ing* to indicate a future action planned by the speaker or writer. *Example:* He is leaving for San Francisco next week.
20. **Future continuous:** *will be + verb + ing* to express a future action occurring within the normal course of events. *Example:* They'll be going to the seashore this summer.
21. **Future perfect:** *will have done* to indicate an action which will be completed by a certain future time. *Example:* We will have done our assignments by next week.
22. **Modals:** *can/could; may/might; shall/should; will/would; must* and *have to* are used.

Reported speech, conditionals, passives and relative clauses are now permitted.

Advanced Stories for Reproduction
American Series

STORY 1 (*p. 2*)

A. 1. Because he was always trying to find good players, but they weren't always smart enough to be accepted by the college.
  2. The dean asked the student what five times seven was.
  3. The student's answer was, "Thirty-six."
  4. The dean threw up his hands and looked at the coach in despair.
  5. The coach said, "Oh, please let him in, sir! He was only wrong by two."
  6. Neither of them was very good at arithmetic.

B. 1. allowed 2. despair 3. persuasion 4. excellent
  5. earnestly

C. 1. confidential 2. confident 3. wooded 4. wooden
  5. imaginative 6. imaginary

STORY 2 (*p. 4*)

A. 1. John was a very lazy boy.
  2. His parents wanted him to be a doctor when he grew up.
  3. John said he wanted to be a garbage collector.
  4. Because he thought he'd only have to work one day a week.
  5. She was very surprised.
  6. Because he saw the ones who came to his house only on Wednesdays.

B. 1. hoped 2. possible 3. bored 4. asked 5. finish
  6. pleasant

C. 1. After watching the garbage collectors on his street, John decided he wanted to become one, too.
  2. Before deciding to become a garbage collector, John did not know what he wanted to be.
  3. While studying at school, John was bored all the time.
  4. John surprised his mother by saying that he wanted to become a garbage collector.

STORY 3 (*p. 6*)

A.
1. One of his uncles, who was rich and had no children of his own, died and left Dave a lot of money.
2. He found a nice office and bought some new furniture.
3. He heard someone coming towards the door of his office.
4. He thought, "It's my first customer!" and quickly picked up the telephone and pretended to be very busy answering an important call.
5. The man knocked at the door, came in and waited politely for Dave to finish his conversation.
6. He said, "I'm from the telephone company, and I was sent here to connect your telephone."

B.

C. hat-rack; chairs; cushions; lampshade; telephone; drill; plaster; paint.

STORY 4 (*p. 8*)

A.
1. Mr. Smith went to and from his office by train every day.
2. A man sitting behind him leaned forward, tapped him on the shoulder and spoke to him.
3. He was reading his newspaper.
4. The man said, "You're not leading a very interesting life, are you?"
5. Mr. Smith asked, "How do you know all that about me?"
6. Because he always sat in the same seat behind Mr. Smith.

B.
1. Mr. Smith did not go to his office on weekends.
2. Mr. Smith went to his office by train five days a week.
4. While he was reading his newspaper one day, he was tapped on the shoulder by another man.
6. The man sitting behind Mr. Smith always saw him in the same seat.
7. The man thought Mr. Smith's life was dull.
10. The man's own life was just as uninteresting as Mr. Smith's.

C.
Sentence 7	Sentence 3	Sentence 2	Sentence 1
Sentence 4	Sentence 8	Sentence 6	Sentence 5

74

STORY 5 (*p. 10*)

A. 1. Lisa went to the mountains for her vacation.
2. Because she hadn't brought enough money.
3. The bank teller asked her to identify herself.
4. Because a lot of people were stealing checkbooks and using them.
5. Lisa felt puzzled.
6. She took her mirror out of her handbag, looked at it, and then said, "Yes, it *is* me."

B. 1. a   2. a   3. a   4. a   5. b   6. a

C. teller; attractive; check; cash; identify; puzzled; vacation; handbag; happily; moment.

STORY 6 (*p. 12*)

A. 1. Shoes and boots were on sale.
2. Because the store wanted to get rid of as many as possible in order to make room for their new stock.
3. Yes, it was.
4. A woman said, "I don't need a bag, thank you. I'm wearing the shoes I bought."
5. The cashier asked her if she would like a bag to put her old shoes in.
6. Because she had just sold her old shoes to someone else.

B. 1. lately   2. late   3. pretty   4. wrong   5. doubly   6. closely

C. 1. c   2. a   3. b   4. e   5. d

STORY 7 (*p. 14*)

A. 1. After Fred had sold the old one.
2. He put a "For Sale" sign in the back window of his car, and another one on the bulletin board in his college dormitory.
3. Because he was driving to another town and he had to pay before being allowed to use the road.
4. He said, "Two dollars and fifty cents."
5. Fred said, "I accept. It's yours." Then he put the car keys into the attendant's hand.
6. No, he didn't.

B. 1. accept   2. surprised   3. allowed   4. entrance   5. value

C. 1. which 2. it 3. X 4. it 5. it 6. where 7. it 8. which
 9. where 10. it

STORY 8 (p. 16)

A. 1. Because he had to walk so much.
 2. Because his doctor told him that salt water was the best thing for them.
 3. He asked him whether he would be allowed to take a bucket of salt water.
 4. He said, "Yes, although you'll have to pay twenty-five cents for it."
 5. He gave the lifeguard twenty-five cents, filled his bucket, took it to his hotel and put his feet in the water.
 6. Because the tide had gone out.
 7. He thought, "That man has a very good business. He must have sold thousands of buckets since this morning."

B. 1. expensive 2. allowed 3. far away 4. lower 5. calm

C. 1. It was very common for doctors to send their patients to the seashore for a rest.
 2. It was stupid of the salesman to ask the lifeguard whether he could take some water.
 3. It was easy for the lifeguard to cheat the salesman.
 4. It was silly of the salesman to think the lifeguard had sold thousands of buckets of water.
 5. It would be impossible for anyone to know so little.

STORY 9 (p. 18)

A. 1. He was asked to give a twenty-minute speech in another city.
 2. His secretary prepared the speech for him.
 3. The audience got very restless and bored by the end of it.
 4. Because the businessman had read the original and the two copies of his speech.
 5. Because she wanted him to check two copies for the files.
 6. He had read the same speech three times.

B.

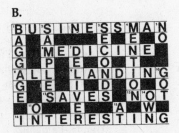

C. speech; audience; beer; wine; bowl; lemon; sandwiches; onion.

STORY 10 (*p. 20*)

A.　1. He pretended that his eyesight was very bad.
　　2. He said, "What chart?"
　　3. He decided that the man's eyes were not good enough for army service.
　　4. The young man went to a movie.
　　5. The doctor who had examined him earlier sat down next to the young man.
　　6. He said, "Excuse me, ma'am, but does this bus go to Main Street?"

B.　1. The young man in this story was unwilling to do his military service.
　　3. He avoided it by pretending that he had bad eyesight.
　　6. When the doctor told him to look at things, he pretended he could not see them.
　　8. He went into a movie theater to see a film.
　10. The doctor came into the theater after the young man.

C.　Sentence 6　　Sentence 2　　Sentence 4　　Sentence 5
　　Sentence 7　　Sentence 3　　Sentence 8　　Sentence 1

STORY 11 (*p. 22*)

A.　1. He was being tested on his knowledge of what to do if someone fell overboard while he was in charge of the ship.
　　2. A big can was thrown into the sea, and he had to pretend it was a man who had fallen in and try to save it.
　　3. The can was pulled under by the ship's propeller.
　　4. He quickly stopped the ship and went backwards.
　　5. He struck the can once more straight in front of the ship.
　　6. A sailor said, "Excuse me, sir, but if I'm ever unfortunate enough to fall into the sea while you're steering the ship, please let me swim to shore by myself!"

B.　1. a　　2. b　　3. b　　4. b　　5. a　　6. a

C. vessel/ship; charge; knowledge; steering; inexperienced; struck; crash; quickly; observing.

77

STORY 12 (*p. 24*)

A. 1. He became a clerk in a big company.
2. He hoped to advance to higher positions as time went on.
3. Because he wasn't very smart.
4. A smart young man, straight from college, joined the same department.
5. He was promoted above Jones.
6. Because he was angry that he hadn't been promoted instead of this young man.
7. Jones said, "I've had sixteen years' experience on this job, yet a new man has been promoted over my head after having been here only one year."
8. The manager answered, "I'm sorry, Jones, but you haven't had sixteen years' experience: you've had one year's experience sixteen times."

B. 1. promoted; interested
2. working; interesting
3. finishing; chosen
4. chosen; promoted
5. talking; experienced

C. 1. c   2. e   3. b   4. a   5. d

STORY 13 (*p. 26*)

A. 1. Because he had never been up in an airplane before and he had read a lot about air accidents.
2. He thought the take-off and the landing were the most dangerous parts of a flight.
3. He was extremely frightened and closed his eyes.
4. He opened them again and looked out of the window of the plane.
5. He said, "Look at those people down there. They look as small as ants, don't they?"
6. The friend answered, "Those are ants. We're still on the ground."

B. 1. frightened 2. finally 3. landing 4. take-off 5. worried
6. boarded 7. closed 8. safe

C. 1. missed 2. spare 3. passing 4. crossing 5. borrow
6. lend

STORY 14 (*p. 28*)

A. 1. Yes, she had one son.
2. The man asked her if her son smoked, drank wine, or came home late at night.
3. She answered "No" to all three questions.
4. He was pleased by her answers.
5. He asked her how old her son was.
6. She answered, "He's six months old today."
7. The man had probably expected the woman's son to be fifteen.

B. 1. soon 2. opposite 3. wise 4. proudly 5. congratulate

C. 1. The woman hadn't been expecting to be questioned about her son, but she was.
2. The man had not expected to have an interesting trip, but he did.
3. The man wasn't expecting the woman's son to be so young, but he was.
4. The woman had not expected to be able to speak proudly of her son, but she was.

STORY 15 (*p. 30*)

A. 1. They were sitting together on a bench in the park.
2. The air was cool and there was moonlight.
3. Her eyes were like bright stars shining in the clear night sky.
4. Her teeth were like pearls reflecting the light of the moon.
5. Her hair was like a golden waterfall in the moonlight.
6. Yes, he did.
7. She said, "Oh, Joe! You say the most wonderful things!"
8. His girlfriend had really been saying all those wonderful things.

B.

C. hay; stream; blades; berries; waterfall; rainbow; lightning; horizon; beam; moonlight.

STORY 16 (*p. 32*)

A. 1. Mr. Grey had a big collection of extremely rare bones.
     2. He managed to get a new and better job at another university.
     3. Because Mrs. Grey had made arrangements for all their possessions to be taken in a moving van to their new home.
     4. He brought out a large wooden box.
     5. He was just about to throw it into the van with all the other things.
     6. She said, "Please treat that box very gently! That one has all of my husband's bones in it."
     7. The man was so surprised that he nearly dropped the box on his feet.

B. 2. Mr. Grey had collected a lot of bones which were very unusual.
     4. He had to move to another town because he was going to work there.
     5. Mrs. Grey watched three men while they took things out of her house and loaded them into a van.
     7. Mr. Grey's collection of bones were in a large wooden box.
     9. The man who was carrying the box was very surprised when Mrs. Grey said it contained her husband's bones.

C. Sentence 5   Sentence 1   Sentence 2   Sentence 4
      Sentence 7   Sentence 3   Sentence 6   Sentence 8

STORY 17 (*p. 34*)

A. 1. He wanted to do some diving in the sea.
     2. He bought a rubber suit and all the other things that he needed, and took some lessons at a diving school.
     3. He saw a lot of beautiful fish.
     4. He saw a man near the bottom of the sea.
     5. He was waving his arms and legs around wildly.
     6. He was wearing only a bathing suit.
     7. He took out a plastic notebook and a special pencil and wrote, "What are you doing here?"
     8. He wrote, "Drowning!"

B. 1. giving; experienced
     2. given; diving
     3. seen; interesting
     4. waving; drowning
     5. made; writing

C. 1. e   2. c   3. d   4. b   5. a

STORY 18 (*p. 36*)

A. 1. Mr. Scott said, "What's wrong with the old one? I can easily fix it."
2. He fixed the vacuum cleaner.
3. This happened again several times.
4. She added a few extra pieces to the pile on the floor.
5. He'd have noticed that they were missing, and would have gone out and bought some more.
6. Because he couldn't find places for all the pieces that were on the floor.

B. 1. fell/went 2. gets 3. goes; comes 4. get 5. fallen
6. come 7. getting 8. went

C. 1. d 2. a 3. e 4. b 5. c

STORY 19 (*p. 38*)

A. 1. She went to live in an attractive village out in the country.
2. She bought her food in the nearest town.
3. The cashier smiled and said, "Good morning, Mrs. Brown."
4. Finally, she said, "Excuse me, but my last name's Green, not Brown."
5. She smiled cheerfully and said, "I'm sorry."
6. She said, "Do you know, Mrs. Brown, there's another lady who comes to our store every Saturday who looks just like you."

B. 1. attractive 2. nearest 3. cheerfully 4. following 5. began
6. convenient

C. 1. known 2. know 3. mentioned 4. discuss 5. go 6. gone
7. delivered 8. to deliver

STORY 20 (*p. 40*)

A. 1. Because Helen was going to have her first baby.
2. She told Sam that he could go home and she would call him when the baby arrived.
3. He said he would rather wait at the hospital.
4. He was walking anxiously up and down in the corridor.
5. She asked, "Which would you have preferred, a boy or a girl?"
6. Because he had an older sister, and she was always very kind to him when he was a child.
7. She said, "Well, it's a boy this time."
8. He answered, "That's all right. That was my second choice."

B. 1. anxiously 2. kind 3. preferred 4. cheerfully 5. older

C. 1. "It's time you went to the hospital," Sam said to Helen.
2. "I wish I had a more comfortable car to take you in," Sam said.
3. "If only you wouldn't (didn't) worry so much!" Helen answered, laughing.
4. Sam would have preferred it if Helen had had a daughter first, but actually she had a son.
5. If there were two babies, they would be company for each other.

STORY 21 (p. 42)

A. 1. It is often very difficult to find someone to come and fix it.
2. Because everybody wants to sell new products, but nobody wants to fix them when they stop working.
3. Because she discovered that her bathroom faucet was leaking.
4. It took him three days to come.
5. She said, "Well, you've finally arrived! I called you *three days* ago."
6. He took a piece of paper out of his pocket and looked at it.
7. He said, "I'm sorry, but I've come to the wrong place. I was looking for Mrs. Smith's house, not yours. *She* phoned me on the 20th."

B.

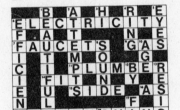

C. electrician; faucets; leak; plumber; pipe; drill; plasters; frames.

STORY 22 (p. 44)

A. 1. He was very unhappy about it.
2. He thought that young people should be taught the difference between right and wrong.
3. He saw some young boys standing around a small cat.
4. He told him, "We're having a contest. We're telling lies, and the one who tells the biggest one gets to keep the cat."
5. He thought that this was a good opportunity to teach the boys a useful lesson.
6. He said, "I've never told a lie in my life."
7. They answered, "You've won! You can take the cat!"

B. 1. The old gentleman was not satisfied with what students were being taught.
   4. He wanted more attention to be paid to morals.
   5. Some boys were having a contest for a small cat in the park.
   8. The biggest liar was going to get the cat.
   10. The old gentleman decided to teach the boys a lesson on morals.
   11. The boys let him have the cat because he had told the biggest lie.

C. Sentence 7   Sentence 1   Sentence 4   Sentence 3
   Sentence 8   Sentence 5   Sentence 2   Sentence 6

STORY 23 (*p. 46*)

A. 1. He found his wife very annoyed about something.
   2. He thought that he was more sensible than his wife.
   3. He started to give her a lecture on the importance of always remaining calm.
   4. He said, "It's a waste of your strength to get excited about small things."
   5. He started shouting, then he jumped up and began to wave his arms around wildly and swear terribly.
   6. Because the thing that landed on his nose hadn't been a fly, it had been a bee.

B. 1. b   2. b   3. b   4. a   5. b

C. annoyed; wave; swear; very; patient; importance; remaining; strength; train; lecture.

STORY 24 (*p. 48*)

A. 1. They were invited to dinner at the home of a college professor.
   2. Because he did not have much education and was afraid that he might make a fool of himself.
   3. He had had a lot to drink and began to get careless.
   4. A guest asked him whether he liked Shakespeare.
   5. He answered, "It's very pleasant, but I prefer scotch."
   6. He said, "You certainly made a fool of yourself making that silly remark about scotch."
   7. His friend thought that Shakespeare was a kind of cheese.
   8. Shakespeare was a famous poet and writer.

B. 1. for going; to persuade   3. about inviting; of being
   2. of his doing; to bring   4. to get; to do

C. 1. b   2. d   3. e   4. a   5. c

STORY 25 (*p. 50*)

A.
1. Senior citizens are allowed to travel cheaply on a bus if they have a special card.
2. She went into town once a week.
3. She usually went by bus.
4. She had to pay the full price for her ride.
5. When she used it for the first time on the bus, it made her feel very old.
6. He said, "Don't forget to give your mother's card back to her when you see her again."
7. Because he noticed that she was feeling unhappy.
8. She was very happy when she heard this.

B.
1. permitted 2. reached 3. cheaply 4. winked 5. unhappy
6. whispered

C.
1. must 2. should 3. must 4. should 5. traveling 6. hurt
7. standing

STORY 26 (*p. 52*)

A.
1. Because he was a very nervous person who always had the convenience of someone else to drive him.
2. He passed his driving test on the second attempt.
3. He was trying to park between two other cars when he damaged one of them slightly.
4. He wrote to the insurance company.
5. They sent him a form to fill in, describing the accident.
6. One of the questions was, "How could the driver of the other car have prevented the accident from happening?"
7. He wrote, "He could have parked his car on another street."

B.
1. nervous 2. prevented 3. pass 4. damaged 5. parking
6. slightly

C.
1. b. Mr. Thompson was sent a form to fill in by the insurance company.
   c. A form was sent by the insurance company for Mr. Thompson to fill in.
2. b. Mr. Thompson was driven around by his mother in her car.
3. b. Cars had been parked, by two people, on the street where Mr. Thompson wanted to park.
4. b. Mr. Thompson caused the accident.

84

5. b. An official examiner had given Mr. Thompson a driving test.
   c. A driving test had been given to Mr. Thompson by an official examiner.

STORY 27 (*p. 54*)

A. 1. Because a lot of movie stars and other famous people ate there, and she was curious to see some of them.
    2. A very attractive man and woman came into the restaurant.
    3. They were beautifully dressed.
    4. She said, "Look at those people, George! I'm sure I've seen their pictures somewhere."
    5. She asked, "Who are those people? Do you know them?"
    6. He answered, "Oh, they're nobody famous."
    7. She said, "Really? How do you know that?"
    8. He told her, "Because they asked me who *you* were."

B.

C. combed; brushed; teeth; nose; jewelry; diamond; necklace; earrings; hat; feather.

STORY 28 (*p. 56*)

A. 1. The artist was a very kind man.
    2. He had forgotten that he did not have any money.
    3. He asked the beggar to have lunch with him.
    4. They went into a small restaurant.
    5. The artist could not pay the bill, so the beggar had to do so.
    6. He said, "Come home with me in a taxi, my friend, and I'll give you back the money for lunch."
    7. He answered, "Oh, no! I had to pay for your lunch, but I'm not going to pay for your taxi home too!"

B. 1. The artist in this story invited a beggar to have lunch with him.
    4. The beggar didn't expect to pay the bill.
    6. The artist wanted the beggar to come home with him by taxi so he could pay him back for the lunch.

7. The artist was going to pay for the taxi ride when he got home.

9. The beggar thought that the artist wanted to have a free taxi ride.

C. Sentence 7   Sentence 1   Sentence 5   Sentence 2
   Sentence 8   Sentence 3   Sentence 6   Sentence 4

STORY 29 (p. 58)

A. 1. When one of them was going to receive his first visit from a new girlfriend.
2. The usual trick was to take all the furniture out of the student's room.
3. Ted Jones was a country boy.
4. He disliked them.
5. He said, "I'm determined that that's not going to happen to me. I'm going to lock my door."
6. They laughed at his confident words.
7. He was astonished to find that all the furniture was there—but the door of his room was gone.

B. 1. a   2. b   3. b   4. a   5. b

C. birthplace; admission; confident; determined; disliked; tricks; laughter; announced; receive; astonished.

STORY 30 (p. 60)

A. 1. George and Carol were studying medicine.
2. They both enjoyed playing jokes on people.
3. Their professors were strongly against it.
4. A skeleton was in one of the lecture rooms.
5. It was there so that the professor could show the students the different bones in the human body.
6. They put a cigarette in the mouth of the skeleton that was to be used for their next lecture.
7. He went up to the skeleton and took the cigarette out of its mouth.
8. He said, "You really should give them up, old boy. Look what they're doing to you!"

B. 1. in; for 2. in; of/about 3. within; of 4. without; to
5. out of; for 6. on; of 7. at; of 8. in; of 9. To; of
10. With; to

C. 1. b   2. e   3. d   4. a   5. c

Oxford 대학출판부/외국어연수사간(한국내 판권 : 외국어연수사에서 보유)
ESL/EFL 교재 저술의 세계적 권위 L.H.Hill 박사의 명저

Stories for Reproduction Series 1~4
이야기의 재현(再現)을 통해 배우는 영어1~4집

■흥미진진한 이야기를 읽거나 듣고 말과 글로 다시 표현해 보는 연습을 통해 표현력(作文·會話)·이해력(讀解·聽解)을 획기적으로 향상시키는 교재

● 이미 40여권의 ESL/EFL(English as a Second/Foreign Language) 교재 저술로 세계적 명성을 떨치고 있는 Leslie A. Hill 박사가 그의 오랜 연구와 교육자로서의 경험을 토대로 최근에 집대성한 영어학습교재의 결정판.

● Hill 박사 특유의 Contextualized Approach(문맥적 접근법)에 토대를 둔 다양한 Oral /Written Reproduction Questions & Exercises(구두 / 필기재현연습)로 표현력과 이해력의 획기적 향상.

● A. S. Hornby 의 Guide to Patterns & Usage in English(25 구문 유형)에 토대를 두고 단어와 구문의 난이도에 따라 상용 기본단어를 4 단계(입문, 초급, 중급, 상급)로 나누어 익히고 활용시키는 교재 총서.

● 영어 실력이 약한 경우는 기초실력 재확립용으로, 어휘력·문법실력이 앞선 경우는 속독력·청해력·작문력·회화력 향상용으로 쓸 수 있는 교재.

● 교실수업, 자습 양용으로 쓸 수 있으며 자습의 경우를 위해 상세하고 친절한 주석과 해답이 담긴 Study Guide와 Answer Key를 마련.

■대학입시·취직시험·각종고시·TOFEL 등 각종 영어 시험 준비용으로 최적.

제 1 집 Introductory, Elementary, Intermediate Advanced Stories for Reproduction 1
　　　　전 4권 Textbook＋Study Guide＋Cassette Pack.

제 2 집 Introductory, Elementary, Intermediate, Advanced Stories for Reproduction 2
　　　　전 4권 Textbook＋Answer Key＋Cassette Pack.

제 3 집 Introductory, Elementary, Intermediate, Advanced Steps to Understanding
　　　　전 4권 Textbook＋Answer Key＋Cassette Pack.

제 4 집 Elementary, Intermediate, Advanced Stories for Reproduction, American
　　　　Series 전 3권 Textbook＋Answer Key＋Cassette Pack.

Oxford대학출판부·외국어연수사간

만화를 즐기며 연마하는 영어 회화 · 작문교재
전 2 권
English through Cartoons
Dialogues, Stories & Questions
Book 1～2
한국내판권보유 : 외국어연수사

유우머와 기지가 넘치는 만화를 즐기면서

(A) **대화**(Dialogues)를 읽거나 테이프를 듣고 영어 특유의
   유우머 감각을 몸에 익히며

(B) 만화를 해설하는 **이야기** (Stories)를 공란을 메우면서 완성하는
   연습을 통해 **작문력**을 기르고

(C) 만화내용의 **질의 응답**을 통해 격조 높은 영어 **회화력**을
   양성하는 영작문 · 회화 연습 교재의 결정판./

● EFL/ESL (English as a Foreign/Second Language) 교재 저술의 세계적 권위
  Leslie A. Hill 박사와 세계적인 만화가 **D. Mallet** 의 최신 역작.

● 폭소와 홍소를 자아내게 하면서도 깊은 뜻을 담은 만화와 대화는 학습상의 긴장을
  덜어 주며 Stories 의 공란을 추리하여 완성토록 유도하는 연습문제와 내용 파악
  질의문은 영어의 **회화력·청취력·작문력·독해력**을 획기적으로 연마·향상.

● 학습 부담을 줄이고 능률을 최대한으로 올리기 위하여 친절하고 자세한 해설과 예문이
  풍부하게 수록된 Study Guide 를 따로 마련.

서강대학교 영어교육연구소 연구협찬/(주) 외국어연수사 간

Common Problems in KOREAN ENGLISH
한국식 영어의 허점과 오류

이 책의 목적은 한국식 영어의 허점과 오류를 바로 잡아주고 「자연스럽고 (natural), 적응성이 풍부하며 (flexible), 관용적인 (idiomatic)」영어 표현을 익히도록 하려는 것이다. 그러므로 이 책은 영어를 자주 써야하는 분들이나 각급학교 영어선생님들과 올바른 영어 표현을 익히고자 하는 학생들에게 유익한 참고서나 길잡이가 될 것이다.

특 색

• 한국식 영어 특유의 오용 사례를 정선한 후 그 원인을 밝혀내어 상세히 설명하고 올바른 표현법을 구체적으로 예시하였다.
• 오용 사례를 (1) 문법적 오류 (2) 낱말 뜻의 혼동 (3) 어색하거나 부적절한 표현의 3편으로 나누어 그 잘못을 지적하고 올바른 문장으로 고쳐 놓았으며, 그 대안으로 다양한 표현방법을 풍부한 예문으로 제시했을 뿐 아니라 방대한 연습문제를 만들고 그 모범답안까지 제시해 두었다.
• 내용설명은 물론 예문과 대화례 (sample sentences and dialogs) 등이 저자 특유의 간명한 필치로 씌어져 있어 이해하기 쉽고 활용도 용이하다.
• 각 문제점의 요점을 간추려 우리말로 옮겨 놓았으며 교실 수업과 자습 양용에 적합하도록 만들었다.

저 자

David Kosofsky는 The University of Maryland에서 서양사를 전공했고(B.A.) Brandeis University에서 비교 역사학을 전공했으며(M.A.) 미국, 일본 및 말레이지아에서 영어를 가르쳤고 1982년에 내한한 이래 서강대학교 영어교육연구소에서 Advanced Seminar class를 가르치면서 영어학습교재의 연구개발에 전념하고 있다. 그는 The Asian Wall Street Journal과 Asiaweek에 기고하면서 소설도 써 왔다.

저자소개

L. A. Hill 박사는 ELT(English Language Teaching)
교재의 저술가로서 그리고 영어 교육계의 세계적인
권위자로 널리 알려진 분으로 그의 저서에는 다음과 같은
것들이 있다.
Stories for Reproduction 1 (전 4 권), Stories for
Reproduction 2 (전 4 권), Stories for Reproduction:
American Series (전 3 권), Steps to Understanding
(전 4 권), Word Power 1500/3000/4500 (전 3 권),
English through Cartoons (전 2 권), Elementary &
Intermediate Composition Pieces (전 2 권), Elementary &
Intermediate Comprehension Pieces (전 2 권),
Intermediate Comprehension Topics, Oxford Graded
Readers (전 4 권), Writing for a Purpose, Note-taking
Practice, A Guide to Correct English & Exercises
(전 2 권), Prepositions & Adverbial Particles &
Exercises (전 2 권), Contextualized Vocabulary Tests
(전 4 권), Crossword Puzzle Book (전 4 권).

Advanced Stories for Reproduction

AMERICAN SERIES

1985년 2월 12일 발행
1996년 3월 31일 초판 2쇄

지은이 L. A. HILL
펴낸이 李 瀅 載
펴낸곳 外國語研修社

판권
본사 소유

서울·영등포구 여의도동 35-2 백상빌딩 1006호
등록 1977. 5. 18 제10-81호
전화 785-0919/785-1749
     780-3644
FAX 780-2817